DIVORCE
AND
THE MILITARY

by

Frank W. Ault
and
Marsha L. Thole

Published by
The American Retirees Association
7564 Trade St.
San Diego, CA 92121-2412

Editor: Ruth B. Haas
Legal Reviewer: James A. Noone
Cover design by Michael Townsend, TechReps, Inc.
Interior design by Marsha L. Thole

This book is not an official publication of the Department of Defense, nor does its publication in any way imply its endorsement by that agency.

Publisher's Cataloging-in-Publication Data
Ault, Frank W. and Thole, Marsha L.
Divorce and the Military
        228 pages. Includes Resources appendix.
        1. Divorce. 2. Military (Family and Divorce). 3. Military Retirement Pay (and Divorce). 4. Law (Domestic Relations). 5. Uniformed Services Former Spouses' Protection Act.
I. Title.
Library of Congress Catalog Card Number: 93-091076
ISBN 0-9639850-0-0 $14.95 Softcover
Printed in the United States of America

Printed in the United States of America
by Desert Dreams Publishers
Albuquerque, NM 87154

DISCLAIMER

This book is designed to provide general information on the issue of nondisability military retirement benefits as a divisible marital asset. It is sold with the understanding that the publisher and authors are not engaged in rendering legal, accounting, or other professional services. State laws relative to domestic relations vary and change frequently. If legal or other expert assistance is required, the reader should consult with competent professionals.

ABOUT THE PUBLISHER

The American Retirees Association (ARA) was chartered in California in 1984 as a nonprofit, tax-exempt corporation to deal with inequities in the Uniformed Services Former Spouses' Protection Act (USFSPA), Public Law 97-252, 10 U.S.C. §1408 *et seq.* Its membership consists of active duty, reserve, and retired members of the uniformed services, both male and female.

The ARA is headquartered in San Diego, California, and maintains an action office in the national capital area. The ARA is recognized, within the national community of veterans' organizations, as the leader of the USFSPA reform effort.

The goals of the ARA are relief for those military veterans already victimized by this unfair law and reduction of the threat to future military retirees. The ARA maintains that there must be fair and equitable treatment for *both* members of any military marriage that ends in divorce.

INTRODUCTION

Making the decision to divorce can be extremely difficult. No one plans, when getting married, to end their marriage. Unfortunately, almost one out of every two marriages in this country ends in divorce, with the divorce rate for military marriages generally mirroring that of the civilian population. As Representative Robert K. Dornan (R-CA) said in a prepared statement before the [then] House Armed Services Subcommittee on Military Personnel and Compensation on April 4, 1990, "There is no stereotype of the ideal military marriage or the unfortunate circumstances that lead to separation."

The Uniformed Services Former Spouses' Protection Act

On September 8, 1982, the Uniformed Services Former Spouses' Protection Act (USFSPA),[1] Public Law 97-252, 96 Stat. 730 (1982), was signed into law. The provisions of the USFSPA are found at 10 U.S.C. §1408 (1982). The effective date was February 1, 1983, but it was made retroactive to June 25, 1981. Courts are authorized to award up to 50 percent of the military member's[2] retirement pay (or up to 65 percent including court-ordered child support) in a divorce.[3]

Original Intent of USFSPA Still Laudatory

The original intent of the USFSPA was laudatory and remains so: to provide, in a divorce action, for the faith-

ful spouse who had loyally supported the military member's career. The American Retirees Association has always advocated traditional support for deserving former spouses, as well as a fair and equitable division of the marital assets. But the USFSPA has created mass confusion in the state courts where decisions based on precedent have, in many cases, resulted in great injustices, primarily due to the myriad of interpretations of the USFSPA, nationwide.

It is not believed that Congress ever envisioned the problems the USFSPA has caused: among them, that it has created, in many cases, another class of victim: the military retiree and his[4] or her current family.

How This Book Came About

This book has come about for two main reasons. First, while there is a lot of information on the USFSPA, the bulk of it was published in the 1982-86 timeframe, primarily in military law publications, law reviews, and family law journals. The military law journals are not readily available to the typical layperson, and even military legal offices do not always carry them. Thus, neither the military member nor the spouse has ready access to the information most needed to learn about and understand how federal law can affect their divorce.

Second, it is not only the experience of the American Retirees Association and its members, but the experience of military spouses as well, that many lawyers know little, if anything, about this law, or worse, do not understand it. Legal counsel's knowledge of this law is, obviously, important to the military member and the spouse. But it should be the cornerstone of an attorney's representation if his or her client is a military member or the spouse of a military member. As part of a military family, the member's or spouse's decision to divorce is complicated by issues (explained in Chapter 8) that civilian couples usually do not have to grapple with. These are issues which arise from circumstances relating to the military member's service.

How You Can Benefit From Reading This Book

Our experience, in hearing from hundreds of military members and their spouses, indicates that the majority of military people have no idea about the law that affects their retired pay in a divorce. And without knowing what the law is and how it could affect your divorce, you run the risk of overlooking the many issues that need to be addressed in your decree, including the appropriate wording. Once the decision to divorce has been made and you begin the process of seeking an equitable dissolution, both your and your attorney's goal should be to:

1. Ensure that the decree will not be reopened due to lack of knowledge or misinterpretation of the USFSPA or the omission of important military issues; and

2. Verify that the coverage of military issues is such that the decree is recognized by the military finance center as being in conformance with the federal law, obviating the need for subsequent modification or clarification.

Why We Wrote the Book—Why Not An Attorney?

Certainly, there are qualified attorneys who could write on this subject (and have). But we wanted to give you some insight from our perspective within the trenches for several reasons.

First, many attorneys have never served in the military and have no idea what it is like to face combat or to be under constraints and restrictions due to military service. And, they often lack knowledge of military benefits and how these benefits are tied to various service requirements. Thus, it is virtually impossible to empathize with the military member's case. Further, lawyer-client communications are often limited because of the adversarial nature of divorces and the myriad of issues associated with a military divorce that are not usually adjudicated in a civilian divorce.

Second, ARA has been on the receiving end of many expressions of dismay over the military divorce process and has heard the problems from all sides (including that of the non-military spouse). From that perspective, we regularly hear the "horror stories" of our military members who occasionally may not have received the best in legal representation. As a result, ARA has taken the lead in seeing that military personnel, Congress, veterans' organizations, and the legal community are kept up to date on the issues surrounding the division of military retired pay in a divorce.

Third, we are rather appalled, not so much at the lack of understanding of the law in this area by military personnel and retirement offices, but by the military services' deliberate omission of it when it comes to informing their personnel of a law which can significantly impact their lives in retirement.

Indeed, military recruits are not briefed on the USF-SPA upon entering the service; nor are those who attend retirement briefings given the information they should have about this law. Consequently, update information has not been provided to military personnel with any degree of regularity. Even many military lawyers, from our experience, do not know the details of this law and, furthermore, they are rarely military divorce specialists who can tell you how the law is being applied in their states, based on *recent* or precedent-setting cases.

If You Are An Attorney Reading This Book

If you are an attorney, you know that the lack of communication is one of the biggest complaints of clients, and, as such, can quickly sour the attorney-client relationship. Divorce is a highly emotional issue for the client, and any miscommunication can aggravate or stall the proceedings for the divorce.

You may or may not have a client who has already gone through the "emotional" divorce and who is now ready to move on with the "legal" divorce. In any case, you are dealing with a military member who has strong emotional ties to the 20 or more years he or she will have served to earn the miliary retired pay. You must be able to appreciate what they went through in the service of their country, as well as the feelings of the spouse who believes that he or she has gone through a lot to earn it, too. Often both parties are dissatisfied with the latitude granted to state courts to treat and divide their assets.

To enhance the flow of information or clear up misunderstandings about military retired pay, you may want to have your client read this book for the basics, and then return to address questions based on their newfound knowledge. By doing so, you will not have to spend your time, or your client's money, to explain the basics. You may find it more efficient to spend your time explaining what you can and cannot do for them, depending on your state's treatment of the USFSPA.

If you are not as familiar with the USFSPA and its implications as you would like to be, or if your client has a unique situation (e.g., a mix of active duty and reserve time), you may want to call the American Retirees Association for references to experienced USFSPA attorneys who work with other attorneys on the specific military aspects of divorce cases.

SBP and Disability

In addition to the USFSPA, two other issues often arise in military divorce cases. These are the Survivor Benefit Plan (SBP) and disability compensation, where non-disability retirement pay is waived to accept VA[5] disability pay.

The SBP is a program designed to provide income protection to spouses, dependent survivors, or former spouses of service members who die in retirement or on active duty after reaching retirement eligibility. SBP is often a complicated negotiating point in divorces because of its cost to the member. It becomes even more so when there is both a former spouse and a current spouse. Eligibility requirements are not as stringent as for retirement pay. Specific information on SBP is available from local military personnel offices (e.g., Personal Affairs Section or the military retirement services officer), and from the Army Air Force Mutual Aid Association (AAFMA)[6] in Arlington, Virginia.

Except for information regarding VA disability as determined by the *Mansell*[7] decision, the reader is encouraged to seek information on VA disability retirement from the local VA medical center and other veterans' organizations, such as the American Legion.

Not only is the VA disability compensation tax exempt, allowing the retiree to take home a greater share of retirement pay[8], but the USFSPA provides that VA disability pay is exempt from inclusion in the disposable retired pay awarded to an ex-spouse in a divorce action. Unfortunately, this prohibition is currently being ignored by some courts.

What This Book Leaves Out

Associated with military retired pay is a host of entitlements, such as the use of military commissaries and exchanges, and access to military medical services. While they are mentioned, they are not covered in any depth, nor the degree to which they may extend to a former spouse or others who may qualify as military dependents. Military legal offices should be able to provide specifics on those entitlements.

The details of various decisions regarding divorce—specific state laws on alimony, child support, and financial planning considerations—are not addressed here. Appendix N lists some sources of that information, free of charge.

One last point needs to be stressed. This book will not have the answer to every question that may arise as you gain knowledge in this area or go through your own divorce. It is not a stand-alone self-help book on how to divorce, or a guide to domestic relations law, or a substitute for consulting an attorney.

This book will, however, provide the information you need to recognize whether the federal law will affect your divorce, how to seek competent professional help, and how to protect yourself.

INTRODUCTION ENDNOTES

1. The abbreviation "USFSPA" will be used to refer to the Uniformed Services Former Spouses' Protection Act. The word "Act" and the abbreviation "FSPA" are also used to refer to this public law.

2. The following terms are used interchangeably throughout this book: military member, member, servicemember, uniformed servicemember, military spouse, spouse, ex-spouse, former spouse.

3. The term "military divorce" has been coined to mean a divorce in which one of the parties is a military member (active duty, reserve, or retired). This term is not legally recognized (a divorce is a divorce), although you will sometimes hear a divorce between a military member and spouse referred to as such for distinction purposes. As used in this book, "military divorce" includes a divorce of a member of *any* of the Uniformed Services.

4. Throughout this book, the impersonal pronouns "he" and "she" are used to refer to either the member or spouse. They are understood to mean "he" or "she." The USFSPA applies equally to male and female members, although the 1980's congressional hearings focused on the spouse who was the "wife."

5. The Veterans Administration was elevated to department level and is now called the Department of Veterans Affairs. The abbreviation "VA" is still used to refer to various veterans benefits and programs.

6. See Appendix N of this book for information on AAFMA.

7. *Mansell v. Mansell*, 104 L.Ed.2d 275, 109 S.Ct. 2023, 10 EBC 2521.

8. A bill was introduced in 1992 that would allow the military retiree to keep the disability compensation without having to forfeit a like amount of regular retired pay. The "concurrent receipt" bill died, but was revived in the 103rd Congress.

CONTENTS

#6—VA disability is not to be divided...#7—Restrictions associated with receiving retired pay apply to the retiree but not the spouse...#8—Civil Service pensions...#9—USFSPA payments survive remarriage of the ex-spouse... #10—Separation bonuses...#11—No statute of limitations.

Truth and consequences...The legal morass...Legal and other precedents...The bottom line.

Female military must get in line behind the nonmilitary wife...DACOWITS...Times have changed...Career discrimination.

Reservists are not always compensated with money...Does the "plight" apply to spouses of reservists...Legal literature lacking...Bottom line for reservists—you are subject to the USFSPA.

"Military" divorce vs. "civilian" divorce...Issues unique to a military divorce...Military benefits an important consideration...20/20/20 and 20/20/15 spouses...Abused Military Dependents Act...Dependent support...SBP—Don't ignore the pre-retirement notification requirements...Social Security...Jurisdiction...Timing can work to both the military member's and spouse's advantage...Do's and don't's... Compliance with the law is in your best interests.

What you need to know if you plan to divorce...General filing and residence requirements...

Service—having divorce papers served...Grounds for divorce...Spousal support...Child support...Property division...Appeal rights...Your base legal office.

The most critical step in your divorce...You are still responsible...Don't go to a lawyer who does not specialize in domestic relations law...Interviewing attorneys... Preparation—what you need to take to the lawyer's office...Basic information...Personal and real property...Financial status...Summary of military service...Preparation is necessary.

Legal and moral obligations in a divorce...Considerations and approaches...Suggested strategies: 1. Get an educated lawyer... 2. The USFSPA is a permissive law... 3. Court rulings on retired pay while on active duty... 4. Do not forget the denominator...5. Know the law regarding disability pay—USFSPA does not award it... 6. Consider the income tax implications... 7. If you were divorced on or prior to June 25, 1981... 8. Avoid windfall benefits... 9. Consider a separation agreement... 10. Don't forget SBP, life insurance, and other survivor benefits... 11. Keep yourself informed... 12. Get organized and know when to cut your losses...One final note about records...Summary.

For the military retiree...For the spouse...April 1990 House hearings and results in the 1991 Defense Authorization Bill...Retroactivity finally laid to rest...Disposable pay redefined for divorces final after February 4, 1991...Protection for abused military dependents and former spouses...Fairness Amendments...What is on the legislative horizon.

1

WHAT YOU DON'T KNOW
CAN
HURT YOU

Imagine for a moment the following scenario:

You were taken prisoner of war and sent to a North Vietnam POW camp from the fall of 1967 until repatriation in 1973—seven years. You were released and returned home only to be served with divorce papers. Then picture being told by a court that it has found that the "date of separation" from your spouse was April 1, 1970, and she did not have to repay any of your pay and allowances that she spent after the date of separation, that she was entitled to your accrued leave pay, monies paid to you under the War Crimes Act for inhumane treatment, and she was entitled to your remaining pay, even though California law stated that earnings and accumulations after the date of separation were separate property. This was on top of the fact that she openly had affairs during the time you spent in the North Vietnam prison. The court also awarded her your home, your car, and 42.7 percent of your military retired pay, and you were ordered to pay child support and spousal support (despite her marriage to one of the attorneys who represented her in the divorce). And, despite your four children all telling the court they wanted to live with you, you received custody of only the two older children.

This, unfortunately, is not the product of someone's imagination. It happened to a military member. Consider the following other actual cases:

A staff sergeant served in combat with the Marine Corps during Operation Desert Storm. Upon return to his duty station in Twenty-Nine Palms, California, with plans to retire with 20 years of honorable military service, he found his wife of 19 years cohabitating with another man. In May 1991 his wife abandoned him and their three children and filed for a no-fault divorce in California. The divorce was final in January 1992, with the spouse receiving half the property of the marriage plus 47.5 percent per month of the sergeant's military retirement pay. The payments will continue until his death or hers, even if she remarries.

A U.S. Marine Corps sergeant major served 25 years in the military. He was married in 1949 and divorced in 1970. The California court found the wife to be an "unfit mother" and awarded custody of the five minor children to the military member (husband). He was married in December 1970 to a woman who also had five children, and they raised all ten. His ex-wife remarried, and then sued in 1987 for retroactive award of his retired pay. In November 1988, the court awarded his ex-spouse 38 percent of his retired pay for life.[1]

An Air Force colonel retired in 1970 after serving 28 years. He was married for 23 years. No retired pay was awarded at divorce, in accordance with the state law. In May 1987 the ex-spouse filed retroactively for (and received) 50 percent of his retired pay. The ex-spouse remarried another military husband; he died and she receives survivor benefits from the second marriage. She was married a third time to a retired USAF officer. The ex-spouse now receives military retired pay from one prior husband and survivor benefits from another, while sharing the retired pay of the third military (retired) member.

An Air Force master sergeant served 20 years in the military, including two tours in Vietnam. He and his wife were married the last 16 years of his military career. While stationed in Alaska, and entering his last year before retirement, he was sued for divorce by his wife (who had found a boyfriend) and thrown out of the house. The Alaska court awarded his ex-spouse 40 percent of his retired pay as property and 27 percent as child support. Out of his monthly $851 retirement check (at the time), he received $130 after taxes. The ex-spouse at the time was making $34,000 a year and living with her boyfriend (who was earning $26,000).

A doctor (lieutenant colonel) in the Air Force who had returned to active duty in 1985 had previously been divorced in Fairfax County, Virginia, in 1980. He remarried and had a second family. At the time, he had been paying alimony of $6,000 per month until he was forced to close his private practice. His ex-wife was employed as a nursing supervisor, earning $35,000 per year, with her own wealth and assets in excess of $2,000,000. In May 1987 his ex-wife garnished his wages for $90,000 per year, with the Fairfax courts stating he had to "keep his ex-wife in the style to which she had become accustomed; that his joining the USAF had made her suffer." There was lack of proper notification and legal representation prior to garnishment.

*The wife of a USAF colonel divorced him in 1964 and remarried shortly thereafter. She was awarded alimony, and received 75 percent of the marital assets. He remarried in 1971 and retired in 1972. The former spouse sued him for arrearages in 1987 plus prospective payments; she requested but was denied an annuity for a like amount of prospective payment for her estate. The military retiree and his second wife of 18 years had already spent $40,000 in legal fees when a judgment was entered in 1989, awarding the former spouse two years' arrearages and 33 percent of **gross pay**[2] for the colonel's life based on his full 30 years' service and subsequent promotion (they were previously married 19 years out of the 21 years of his active duty time at the time of separation).*

Unfair but Legal

If these cases sound unfair or outrageous to you, please be advised that they are entirely legal and strictly routine for Vietnam, Desert Storm, and other military veterans. Most veterans have not been informed by their military leadership about a law that will materially reduce the amount of military retired pay they will receive. Whether they are retired and already receiving retirement pay or on active duty and expecting to receive full retirement pay, they need to be informed about this law.

Treatment of Retired Pay—the Result of Two Major Legal Actions

In accordance with federal law, divorce courts may treat military retired pay as a marital property asset. Worse, it may be treated in a divorce either as property or as income, or both, and be subject to division, with a subsequent award to the ex-spouse. This unique treatment of military retired pay is the result of two major legal actions.[3]

The first is the U.S. Supreme Court decision in *McCarty v. McCarty* (453 U.S. 210 [1981]). On June 26, 1981, the Court ruled that "the military retirement system confers no entitlement to retired pay upon the retired member's spouse and does not embody even a limited community property concept." The court further stated that "the application of community property principles to military retired pay threatens grave harm to clear and substantial Federal interests." In its decision, however, the court recognized that the situation of an ex-spouse of a retired military member could sometimes be a serious one, possibly resulting in destitution or some other unfair predicament, and invited Congress to legislatively review and change the situation.

And change the situation it did. Congress inserted a rider to the Defense Authorization Act for FY 1983, which is known as the Uniformed Services Former Spouses' Protection Act (USFSPA). This public law (97-252) was passed in September 1982, with an effective date of February 1, 1983, and backdated to June 25, 1981, one day before the *McCarty* decision. Thus, the USFSPA circumvented but did not supersede the *McCarty* ruling by providing that "a (state) court may treat disposable retired pay payable to a (military) member for pay periods beginning after June 25, 1981, either as property solely of the member or as property of the member and his[4] spouse in accordance with the law of the jurisdiction of such court."

States Had Already Been Dividing Retired Pay in Divorces

Up until this time, some states had already been including and treating military retired pay the same way they treated civilian pensions, and making an award of this marital asset to the spouse. Now, with the passage of the USFSPA, the state courts could treat military retired pay as both pay and property, using it, in addition, as a source for alimony as well as child support.

Although you may conclude after reading this book that the *McCarty* decision should go down in history as one of the more important decisions of the Supreme Court, we must report that it did not make the top 100.[5] (It didn't make the court's 10 worst decisions, either.) The intricacies of a "military" divorce and division of military retirement benefits are usually neither known nor understood by military people who first contemplate divorce. Moreover, knowledge of *McCarty* and its consequences is not widespread in the civilian legal community or in

Congress. This makes it imperative that you be informed yourself. This book has been written to do just that.

Problems Not Foreseen

Many military members do not think that Congress envisioned the problems that are now occurring. The USFSPA states that state courts *may* divide a military member's retirement pay in a divorce action. But, in reviewing its 11-year history, the USFSPA has operated in *theory* as an *option*, but, in *practice*, as a *mandate*. Its track record provides irrefutable evidence that the USFSPA unfairly discriminates against divorcing military members who manifestly do not enjoy protection under the law equal to that provided their civilian counterparts. So long as courts continue to automatically make lifetime awards of military retirement pay to former spouses, regardless of whether the ex-spouse remarries or is financially or economically stable, the courts will continue to create a class of victims other than the spouses it was designed to assist: the military retiree and his or her current family.

We realize that for every "horror" story military members can cite, former spouses' groups can cite one, too. Nevertheless, honorable military veterans have never subscribed to the theory of the "throwaway spouse" and readily agree that the proper goal of a divorce settlement is the fair and equitable treatment of *both* members of a military marriage, with the recognition, as well, of nonmonetary contributions of both parties. The American Retirees Association (ARA) believes that this is possible, even in the era of the no-fault divorce, and taking into account the substantial social, economic, and cultural changes that have altered the status of military families since the early 1980s.

CHAPTER ENDNOTES

1. Up until November 1992, a former spouse could petition a court to reopen the divorce case to apply for retroactive division of the retired pay if the divorce occurred before June 25, 1981. This loophole was closed with the passage of Public Law 101-510, §555 in November 1990. The case is used as an illustration of the inequities that existed in the USFSPA, and to show that, with perserverance, a law can get changed.

2. At the time, the federal law allowed for an award of only *net disposable retired pay.*

3. Another very important decision handed down by the U.S. Supreme Court in 1989, *Mansell v. Mansell*, exempted disability pay, waived in lieu of retired pay, from being divided in a divorce.

4. The USFSPA applies equally to male *and* female military members.

5. Reference is made to the recently published book, *The Supreme Court: A Citizen's Guide,* by Robert J. Wagman (New York: Pharos Books, 1993). The book cites the 100 most significant decisions the court has made.

2

WHAT USFSPA IS AND WHAT IT IS NOT

Many military members are either uninformed or ill informed when it comes to the provisions of the Uniformed Services Former Spouses' Protection Act. As a result, they can get "blindsided" by not knowing what this law means to them. Thus, some discussion of basic precepts is in order. Subsequent chapters of this book elaborate on those concepts.

What Does the USFSPA Do?

Simply stated, this federal law authorizes state courts to treat military retired pay as property and to award up to 50 percent of it to a former spouse in a divorce.

Who USFSPA Applies To

USFSPA is applicable to both male and female members of the uniformed services, regular and reserve, who

are on active duty, in the reserves, or already retired, in the following:
- Army
- Navy
- Air Force
- Marine Corps
- Coast Guard
- National Guard and Reserve
- Public Health Service
- National Oceanographic and Atmospheric Administration.

Where USFSPA Applies—Locations

USFSPA is applicable in any court of competent jurisdiction in the following:
- The 50 states
- District of Columbia
- Commonwealth of Puerto Rico
- Guam
- American Samoa
- Virgin Islands
- Northern Mariana Islands
- Trust Territory of the Pacific Islands
- Any foreign country with which the United States has an agreement to honor its court orders.

USFSPA Characteristics

The basic characteristics of USFSPA are as follows:
- Applies to all military divorces* subsequent to June 25, 1981.

---

* "Military divorce" is the term used throughout this book to define a divorce between a member of any "uniformed service" and his or her spouse (who may or may not also be a military member).

- Prohibits some, but not all, retroactive awards of military retired pay prior to June 25, 1981.
- Permits military retired pay to be classified as **property** for purposes of a divorce settlement.
- Permits the ex-spouse to receive up to 50 percent of the military member's retired pay, based on the number of years married concurrent with military service.
- Ignores fault, merit, need, ability to pay, or respective final circumstances.
- Prohibits courts from ordering a military member to retire in order to commence USFSPA payments.
- Does not allow courts to order a military member to begin making USFSPA payments before the member has actually retired.
- Requires the establishment of a court's jurisdiction for a partitioning under the USFSPA.
- For divorces final before February 5, 1991, it defines "disposable pay" as the total monthly pay, less:
    - existing debts to the government
    - waivers for VA disability or Civil Service pay
    - SBP premiums when the former spouse is the beneficiary
    - amounts withheld for federal, state, or local income taxes.
- For divorces final on or after February 5, 1991, "disposable pay" has been redefined and *does not* include subtractions for personal debts or taxes.
- Provides for payments of retired pay to the abused ex-spouses of military personnel whose entitlement to retirement pay has been terminated or denied.

No-Fault Feature

- The military member appears to wear the "black

hat"—i.e., the member is considered to be at fault, given that the award of military retired pay (as defined in the federal law) is not based on merit, need, or ability to pay.

Misconceptions about USFSPA

Many military members are ill informed or uninformed when it comes to the applicability of the USFSPA. *Many military members wrongly believe that the USFSPA:*

- Returned a "pre-existing right" to the states.

  As confirmed by *McCarty*, the states did not have such authority prior to the USFSPA. The USFSPA now allows the state courts to consider military retired pay in the same way they apply state law to other "pension plans."

- Is automatically a part of the military divorce process.

  Just as the state courts retain authority to establish settlement agreements involving other property and income, they retain the right to determine whether military retired pay should be included or excluded as property of either party.

- Precludes the court from concurrently ordering alimony or child support.

  Since the state may treat the military retired pay as "property," a state could exclude it from consideration as a source of alimony and child support *in addition to* the award of the retired pay. Unfortunately, the award of the share of the military retired pay does not preclude the contemporaneous award of alimony or child support payments, or both, whether or not retirement pay is the only source for these payments.

- Applies only to male military members.

  While it is true that male military members significantly outnumber the female members, USFSPA is gender neutral and applies equally to both sexes.

- Does not apply to Reserves (and Guard).

  This law applies to active duty, retired, and reserve/guard (whether active duty, inactive status, or retired), pay and nonpay categories.

- To qualify for payments, the benefitting ex-spouse must be married to the military member at least 10 years.

  The marriage need not have lasted ten years for the spouse to acquire a share of or interest in the military member's retired pay. The marriage *does*, however, need to have lasted 10 years (during 10 years of creditable military time) in order for the ex-spouse to receive a direct payment (irrevocable) from a defense finance center.

- Permits partitioning of active duty pay prior to retirement.[1]

  The USFSPA does not apply to active duty pay. A court, however, can order the active duty military member to pay alimony or other support, including child support, from whatever source it deems appropriate, and then order the commencement of USFSPA payments upon retirement.

- Includes partitioning of disability pay.

    The USFSPA prohibits the partitioning of certain disability pay. Moreover, the U.S. Supreme Court confirmed in the *Mansell* decision that military disability pensions are not marital property subject to division. However, the member's disability pay is being divided by some state courts,[2] in violation of that Supreme Court decision and, indeed, the provisions of the USFSPA itself.

- Is in addition to Survivor Benefit Plan premiums.

    The award of the Survivor Benefit Plan (SBP) to a former spouse is exclusive from an award of retired pay under USFSPA. In other words, an ex-spouse might not get any portion of the retired pay but might be named as the SBP beneficiary (as could children and others). SBP premiums are, however, deductible from the amounts involved in USFSPA payments to the same ex-spouse.

- Is the only recourse of the spouse of a military member in a divorce proceeding.

    Individuals married to military members have always had (and still have) access to all the remedies and protections available to non-military couples in divorce court.

Problems and Pitfalls

The military is unique and not just for its mission. Just as the military is singled out in a number of ways, some positive and some not so positive [e.g., frequently proposed cost-of-living-allowance (COLA) reductions in retired pay], so it has been with the USFSPA. These issues, as listed below, are explained further in Chapter 3.

- This law was not grandfathered.
- Payments continue after remarriage of the former spouse.
- USFSPA does not preclude contemporaneous awards of alimony, child support, or other support.
- USFSPA provides windfall benefits to the ex-spouse, often at the expense of a second spouse who has been married to the military member longer than the first spouse was.
- USFSPA does not preclude further garnishment of the military member's pay.[3]
- The military member has continuing federal obligations; the benefitting ex-spouse does not.[4]
- There is no statute of limitations on when the former spouse must file to receive the retired pay.

Two other problems need to be highlighted, as they have perhaps the greatest potential for negatively affecting the military member's retired pay in a divorce:

- Military members are not being informed of this law.
- The civil legal community is generally not familiar with this law.

It is important to know how this law can affect your retired pay, and that the courts can give lifetime awards of a part of your military retirement pay to your former spouse, based on your pay grade at retirement and *not at the time of divorce*, regardless of whether the ex-spouse remarries or is financially or economically stable. The next chapter addresses the various implications and problems that have arisen as a result of this law.

CHAPTER ENDNOTES

1. A recent (July 1993) New Mexico court decision, *Ruggles v. Ruggles*, has ruled that a spouse can be awarded immediate payment of a *vested* pension, even though the other spouse has not begun receiving it. This applies to military retirement. While this appears to violate and preempt federal law, until a military divorce case is appealed in New Mexico, we do not know what impact this decision will have on other military divorces where the member has not yet retired. Given the defense drawdown and restructuring, a 20-year career is no longer guaranteed.

2. Again, New Mexico is one of those states where courts have divided disability pay in violation of the *Mansell* decision.

3. The only disability pay protected by the USFSPA is that awarded under Title 61 of the U.S. Code, where the military retiree waives a portion of his or her retired pay in order to receive equivalent compensation from the Department of Veterans Affairs. Pursuant to 42 U.S.C. §659 through 662, et seq., certain classes of disability pay *can* be garnished to provide child support or make alimony payments.

4. Over 4000 retired military members were recalled to active duty during Operation Desert Storm. USFSPA beneficiaries were not subject to (recall to) active duty.

3

WHERE WERE YOU IN '82 (THINGS YOUR RECRUITER DIDN'T TELL YOU)

Historical Look at Community Property

First, a short historical look at the subject of community property.[1,2] In earlier times, the man typically owned and controlled the wealth in a marriage. A divorce could leave the wife in a destitute state, and often did. Recognizing this unfairness, state laws gradually came to include a more balanced view of the assets acquired in a marriage. The concept of recognizing that each party contributes to the marriage is treated somewhat differently in each state; however, it can generally be said that states are either community property states (i.e., each party has a 50-50 property right to all that was acquired during the marriage) or adhere to a principle of equitable interest/distribution (may not necessarily be 50-50, but it is equitable).[3]

Just because one party brings home the paycheck does not mean the other party's nonmonetary contributions do not deserve to be recognized. The Maryland courts have addressed this subject head-on:

> *The Commission does not believe that the people of Maryland today hold the view that a spouse whose activities within the marriage do not include the production of income has never contributed anything toward the purchase of property acquired by either or both spouses during the marriage. Its members believe that non-monetary contributions within a marriage are real and should be recognized in the event that the marriage is dissolved or annulled. As homemaker and parent and housewife and handyman (of either sex), as a man and a woman having equal rights under the law united into one family unit, in which each owes a duty to contribute his or her best efforts to the marriage, the undertakings of each are for the benefits of the family unit. In most cases, each spouse makes a contribution entitled to recognition, even though the standards or methods of quantifying a spouse's non-monetary contribution are inexact.*[4]

Tracing the history[5] of the matter of military retirement benefits as an asset in a divorce is not easy. Thus, only a narrative summary is presented here.

Landmark McCarty Decision—Precursor to the USFSPA

On June 26, 1981, the U.S. Supreme Court ruled 6-3, in *McCarty v. McCarty*, 453 U.S. 210 (1981), that federal law precluded the award of military nondisability retirement benefits as marital property upon divorce because a conflict was found between the property right issue for the spouse and the federal interests in the military retirement statutes. The issue was whether federal statutes granting nondisability military retirement benefits preempted California courts from dividing such benefits upon divorce.

The court's own words, in holding that federal law precludes a state court from dividing military retired pay according to state community property laws, were:

> *There is a conflict between the terms of the federal military retirement statutes and the community property right asserted by the appellee. The military retirement system confers no entitlement to retired pay upon the retired member's spouse, and does not embody even a limited community property concept. Rather the language, structure, and history of the statutes make it clear that retired pay continues to be the personal entitlement of the retiree.*

> *Moreover, the application of community property principles to military retired pay threatens grave harm to clear and substantial federal interests...In addition, such a division has the potential to interfere with the congressional goals of having the military retirement system serve as an inducement for enlistment and re-enlistment and as an encouragement to orderly promotion and a youthful military.*

There followed much turmoil, as many retirees quit paying former spouses the "community property" share of their military retirement pay. Concomitantly, state courts, citing concepts of *res judicata*,[6] denied any application for cases already decided. Outraged ex-spouses had military members ordered back into court to make up and continue payments as well as to pay court costs and legal fees for both sides. Federal courts denied jurisdiction and appeals courts supported the divorce courts. For divorces during this period, the state courts had no choice but to find that the military retired pay was not community property.

Thus, the *McCarty* decision was not without controversy, with cries of unfairness not only from the military retiree but by the nonmilitary spouse of long-term marriages, and a "taking back" from the states of the power and authority (they had assumed they had) to divide military retirement benefits.

Supreme Court "Invites" Congressional Action

In the *McCarty* decision, the court "invited" congressional action, by making it clear that the source of any change in military retirement policy rested with Congress. The outcome of efforts to overrule *McCarty* was the signing into law on September 8, 1982, of the Uniformed Services Former Spouses' Protection Act,[7] Public Law 97-252, 96 Stat. 730 (1982). The provisions of the USF-SPA, which counteract the *McCarty* decision, are found in 10 U.S.C. §1408 et seq. (1982). The effective date was February 1, 1983, but it was made retroactive to June 25, 1981, one day prior to the *McCarty* decision.

While the *McCarty* decision addressed only community property principles applicable to military retirement, it has been for all intents and purposes applicable to the division of marital property in equitable distribution jurisdictions. Our research has shown, however, that the more complicated, controversial, and complex cases have come out of California and Texas (both community property states), states where there is a heavy military representation, both active duty and retired. One must understand, however, that *McCarty* did not permit either community property or equitable distribution jurisdictions to classify military nondisability retirement pay as community or marital property. And the USFSPA does not impinge on *McCarty* in that it does not prevent a court from awarding alimony or child support, or both, in addition to the retirement benefits.

USFSPA presents some unique situations because of the dates for the U.S. Supreme Court decision, the passage of USFSPA, and the retroactivity of USFSPA. Application of the law varies on when the divorce took place and whether the disposition of military retirement benefits was decided at that time. Thus, a case (up until the 1990 change to the law) may be decided based on (1) pre-*McCarty* state law (before June 26, 1981); (2) modification of a prior favorable judgment, due to a retroactive application of *McCarty*; (3) the gap period (the 19-month period from June 1981 to February 1983) during which federal law preempted state community property laws; or (4) retroactive application of USFSPA to allow the division of benefits paid during all pay periods after June 25, 1981 (the day before the date of the *McCarty* decision).

Mass Confusion in State Appellate Courts

Both *McCarty* and USFSPA created mass confusion in the appellate courts, and decisions based on precedent were, in many cases, ignored, primarily due to myriad interpretations given to *McCarty* and USFSPA. Retroactivity was extensively litigated (and still is today, but much less than before). USFSPA did not prohibit the reopening of cases, it merely permitted state courts to reconsider judgments in light of marital property and procedural laws without the presence of *McCarty*.

A cursory review of any cases in any state code will show that, nationwide, courts of appeals in the same state have taken almost as many different approaches to the problems of adjudicating military retirement benefits during the problematic *McCarty*-era and post USFSPA-era as there are reported cases on the subject.

How the Law Was Passed

The USFSPA permits the states to treat the military retired/retainer pay as they treat civilian pensions, with certain exceptions. The Act attracted little attention at the time it was passed, probably because it was a rider to the annual Department of Defense Authorization Bill.

Sponsored by Rep. Patricia Schroeder (D-CO), the bill was intended to help former spouses left destitute by their military mates and to repay them for years invested in helping the spouse's military career. It has done the opposite in many cases, creating hardships for military members and their second families.

Many felt this law was unnecessary. Military spouses have always had the same range of divorce remedies as any other spouses, including garnishment of pay. Now, the military member feels as if he or she is being blamed for the breakup of the marriage. There is no requirement for the spouse to prove economic or financial need, or "contribution to the military member's career." Moreover, the law can (and has) "reward(ed)" miscreant spouses.

Unlike other retirement plans, the military plan has unique requirements. In order to receive the retired/retainer pay, the military member must have served no less than 20 years of active creditable service. For the former spouse to receive direct payment (from the service accounting and finance center) of up to 50 percent (65 percent to honor a garnishment for child or spousal support) of the disposable net retirement pay, the marriage need only have lasted at least 10 years (during which the member performed at least 10 years of creditable service).

The division of pay is considered separate from any alimony or child support. Further, the pay continues even after remarriage of the former spouse (unlike alimony and most other forms of spousal support). This has not precluded the states from awarding other amounts (including half of the retirement pay) in cases where the military marriage lasted less than 10 years.

Post-USFSPA Enactment Problems Not Envisioned

Military members do not think that Congress envisioned the problems that are now occurring. By automatically allowing lifetime awards of the military retirement check to former spouses, regardless of whether the ex-spouse remarries or is financially or economically stable, Congress has created a situation where it is possible that the military member will become the one who is destitute, particularly when the divorce case is reopened and benefits applied retroactively.

As you will see in Chapter 12, nothing happened in Congress to change the law from 1982 forward until 1989 (with the exception of changes to 10 U.S.C. § 1448 et seq., the Survivor Benefit Plan).

CHAPTER ENDNOTES

1. In researching this subject, one may find references to its similarity with the pension laws of the Foreign Service and Central Intelligence Agency. These two federal agencies' retirement plans are not addressed here.

2. Please note that this book addresses primarily the issue of nondisability military retirement benefits as divisible marital property.

3. Only an in-depth study of the results of a society with many two-income families could determine whether the concept of 50-50 should be more universally applied.

4. Report of The Governor's Commission on Domestic Relations Laws, at 3 (1978), as quoted in *Harper v. Harper*, 284 Md. 54, 448 A.2d 916, 920 (Md, 1982).

5. Prior to 1975 the federal government did not get involved in divorces vis-a-vis military retirement. In 1973, Rep. Patricia Schroeder (D-CO) drafted legislation that became Public Law 93-647 and attached it to the Social Security Act. It allowed state courts to garnish active and retired pay for child support. In 1975 section 459 was effective to provide for garnishment of retirement pay for alimony. Public Law 95-30 limited the amount of retirement pay that could be garnished. Public Law 95-366 authorized the assignment of retirement pay of a civilian employee to a former spouse in a community property settlement. In 1981 Rep. Schroeder proposed H.R. 3039 and H.R. 1711 for court-awarded military retirement benefits. Senator Dennis DeConcini (D-AZ) proposed S. 1453 to distribute military retirement benefits following divorce.

6. *Black's Law Dictionary, Abridged 5th Edition* defines *res judicata* as: A matter adjudged; a thing judicially acted upon or decided; a thing or matter settled by judgment. Rule that a final judgment rendered by a court of competent jurisdiction on the merits is conclusive as to the rights of the parties and their privies, and, as to them, constitutes an absolute bar to a subsequent action involving the same claim, demand or cause of action.

7. This has sometimes been known as the "Schroeder Amendment," as it was initially introduced and sponsored by Rep. Patricia Schroeder.

4

CONTROVERSY
APLENTY

Background

On the surface, it would not appear that the basic thrust of the USFSPA—allowing state courts to treat the military retired/retainer pay as they treat civilian pensions, with certain exceptions—would create problems. The law that was enacted was intended to help former spouses left "destitute" by their military mates and to repay them for years invested in helping the spouse's military career. Unfortunately, it has done the opposite in many cases.

The unique characteristics of military retired pay have created a number of controversies surrounding the USFSPA, as shown below, many of which have been cited in divorce case appeals. It is not our intent to resolve these controversies by discussion in this book, but rather to make you aware that they have and continue to create problems as they are interpreted by each court. Further, while courts have usually rendered decisions based on "precedent," this has not always been the case, even within the same jurisdiction, when it comes to military divorce judgments.

Controversy #1 — Definition of Retired Pay and Its Treatment by the Courts

Perhaps the most talked about controversy is the anomaly created by the definition of military retired pay. The Department of Defense views military retired pay as reduced pay for reduced services. Military retired pay is defined in federal statutes as income; it is treated as income in a tax court; and it is treated as income in a bankruptcy court. But for purposes of USFSPA, state courts *may* treat it as property in a divorce action. Nowhere in statute or case law is military retirement compensation defined as either a pension or as property. One way to look at this controversy from the other side, and one of the ways it was seen when the law was enacted, is that military retirement pay is often the only major asset that a military couple has. Military members in earlier days moved from one base or post to another every two years or so, making the acquisition of a house or other tangible marital assets somewhat out of the question.

This unique treatment of *military* retired pay is, to be sure, just that. No comparable federal law for non-military former spouses exists. Indeed, Congress grandfathered certain employees in the Foreign Service and Central Intelligence Agency for similar retirement programs. Payments to those former spouses do not come out of the retiree's retirement check. Rather, payments are made by the federal government.

Controversy #2 — Retroactivity (still causing problems)

Another controversy that has been addressed by Congress, but not necessarily ended, is that of retroactivity. USFSPA did not grandfather any military member who had been divorced prior to the enactment of the law. (Congress did, however, grandfather retirees in six other federal retirement programs.) This meant that the law changed *after* many military members had already retired. Thus, a military member who had been retired, for example, for 15 years, and perhaps remarried with a second family, might find himself or herself facing a judgment for back retired pay plus half of all future retired pay. Because grandfathering was not done, some retirees were forced into bankruptcy as the state courts applied this law retroactively and required the payment of arrearages.

While it is not unusual for Congress to *not* grandfather every piece of legislation, in this case Congress stated, in a conference report, that the USFSPA was not intended to allow courts to reopen divorce cases. Unfortunately, that statement was not codified into the law itself. Much to the surprise of Congress and state courts, former spouses did, indeed, suddenly reappear with court orders and judgments for arrearages and prospective retired pay. Retroactive reopenings or partitionings were finally halted with the passage in November 1990 of Public Law 101-510, Section 555.

Even then, however, the 1990 amendment required military members to continue to make USFSPA payments for a period of two more years (until November 5, 1992) before they were relieved of the problem of retroactive reopenings. Worse, the 1990 amendment did not apply to divorces prior to *McCarty* wherein an award of retirement pay had already been made or a court had reserved jurisdiction over a future distribution of retired pay.

The problem of retroactivity was never foreseen. Indeed, in a letter to the ARA Executive Director, Lawrence J. Korb (former Assistant Secretary of Defense), acknowledged that "it was not [his] view nor that of DOD that such a law be allowed to be retroactive in its application, and it was [his] understanding that grandfathering was, in fact, incorporated from the start to prevent after-the-fact disenfranchisement of military personnel."[1]

Although payments on some retroactively reopened cases ceased in November 1992, retroactive applications of the USFSPA are still causing problems because some state courts are ignoring the 1990 amendment to the USFSPA.[2] Moreover, as mentioned above, the law provided no relief in the case of those pre-*McCarty* divorces where retirement pay had already been awarded or jurisdiction to award had been retained by the court.

Controversy #3 — Treatment Disparate from Other Federal Retirement Programs

A third controversy is that of the disparity between the military and their retired pay and that of other groups of federal employees and their retired pay. For example, CIA and Foreign Service retirees were grandfathered when similar legislation was passed that affected the division of retired pay in a divorce settlement. Requirements for spousal support under those systems included filing limitations, no retroactivity, and termination of payments upon remarriage before a certain age.

Controversy #4 — The Spouse Is Always Treated as the "Innocent" Party

Another controversy that causes military members a lot of consternation is that the law implies that it is the spouse who is the "innocent" party and the military member who is the "heavy," or guilty party. Just as it is not always the military member who is the plaintiff in a divorce action, so it is not always entirely the member's "fault" in the breakup of a marriage. USFSPA, however, allows the states to ignore fault or need in rendering awards and, in fact, often "rewards" miscreant spouses.

Controversy #5 — Award of Retired Pay Based on Rank at Retirement, Not at Time of Divorce

A continuing controversy, and one of the main objectives of attempts to amend the USFSPA, is that it does not specify that the computation and subsequent award of retired pay is to be based on the rank/pay grade of the member at the time of the divorce. This is illustrated in the following example:

> *The military member, who is a captain (O-3) at the time of divorce, is divorced at the 10-year point. Assume that Spouse Number 1 is awarded 50 percent of his retired pay in the divorce settlement. There are no children. He remarries at the 13-year point, has two children, and continues to serve for a total of 30 years. He retires at the rank of colonel (O-6). It could certainly be said that Spouse Number 2, if you interpret the original intent of USFSPA, "contributed" more to his career than did Spouse Number 1, by virtue of having been married to him longer (17 years vs. 10 with the first wife).*
>
> *Yet, as a result of USFSPA, the finance center will compute the share of retired pay to Spouse Number 1 at the rank of colonel, not captain.[3] Spouse Number 2 and the children are the ones who are shortchanged here. What did spouse Number 1 do to contribute to his career after they were divorced? The answer is "nothing."*

Thus, courts generally have interpreted the law to read that the amount to be awarded to the former spouse is to be based on the military member's rank and years of service at the time of retirement. Only infrequently have courts said it is to be calculated on the basis of the date of the divorce. The argument is that an ex-spouse is unfairly benefitting from the increased retirement pay as a result of longevity or promotions. Indeed, if a second spouse has been married to the member longer than the first spouse, it could be the second spouse who has "contributed" more to the member's career than the former spouse.

Controversy #6 — VA Disability Is Not to be Divided

Some courts, in violation of the U.S. Supreme Court decision in *Mansell*[4] and, indeed, the USFSPA itself, are dividing the military member's disability compensation (received from the Veteran's Administration in lieu of regular retired pay). VA compensation is exempt under Federal law from being divided and the Supreme Court has confirmed that military disability pensions are not marital property subject to division.

Several efforts in Congress to introduce bills that would allow the retiree to receive the VA compensation in addition to the regular retired pay have met with little success. The Department of Defense is opposed to concurrent payment. You may wish to contact your representatives in Congress to see where they stand on this issue.

Controversy #7 — Restrictions Associated with Receiving Retired Pay Apply to the Retiree but Not to the Spouse

Further adding to the debate on this issue are a host of duties, obligations, and restrictions to which the military retiree is subject. You will find these in the "small print" in the papers you receive when you retire. For starters, retirees are subject to recall to active duty (physical condition permitting). They also remain subject to the Uniform Code of Military Justice (UCMJ) and are restricted in certain post-service activities. Contingency Mobilization Plans include the recall of between 22 and 86 percent of the retired force, depending on the service. In other words, retired members continue to serve.

Other restrictions pertain to employment. Retirees who want to accept employment with a foreign government are required to have prior approval of the Secretary of State and the service secretary. Acceptance without approval would result in reduction or forfeiture of retired pay. In addition, a retiree is forbidden to accept employment with a defense contractor within three years of retirement if the member worked on projects that the contractor was also engaged in.

Based on their active duty assignments, some retirees are restricted from traveling to specific foreign countries without prior approval from the service secretary. Again, they are subject to the UCMJ if they violate such orders.

The remaining restrictions have to do with dual compensation limits on federal employment salary, publishing military experiences, lecturing on sensitive military subjects, wearing of the uniform and medals, and conduct while in uniform.

Ironically, the former spouses, who are drawing from the same retirement pay envelopes, are not subject to any of the above obligations or restrictions. Indeed, the nonmilitary spouse frequently has more right to military retired pay than a military spouse of a military member.[5] Specifically, an ex-spouse may be entitled to the military member's retirement pay after a marriage of any length. Unless divorced, a military spouse married to a military member has to serve at least 20 years to qualify for military retirement pay on his or her own.

Controversy #8 — Civil Service Pensions

Questions have arisen as to how the divorce decree is enforced when the military retiree returns to work for the federal government. Oftentimes, it is impossible to know whether the military member will ever work for the government, particularly when the member is still on active duty. What happens when the retiree combines his military time with a civil service pension? How is the aspect of dual compensation[6] treated, where the retiree (if a regular officer) must forfeit $1 for every $2 earned over a certain amount, and on which the pay is capped? Some circumstances can be foreseen, others cannot. To try to compensate for every situation would be cumbersome, not to mention the calculation problems that would ensue.

Logically, ex-spouses could expect their USFSPA payments to be reduced proportionate to the reduction in military retirement pay experienced as a result of dual compensation statutes. However, this could probably be contested if the USFSPA payment appeared in the divorce decree as a finite amount, rather than a percentage. Since there is no law covering the impact of dual compensation laws and USFSPA payments, litigation in this arena could become commonplace.

Controversy #9 — USFSPA Payments Survive Remarriage of the Ex-Spouse

Since its enactment in 1982, the USFSPA has contained no provision terminating payments of retired pay to former spouses despite the remarriage of those former spouses. This is unfair to retired military members for the following reason:

> *It discriminates against retired military members in that it is inconsistent with the treatment of former spouses under all other Federal government retirement and survivor benefit systems.*

This disparate treatment of the military is illustrated below. The remarriage consideration is included in all other Federal retirement benefit programs, thereby discriminating against military members.

Retirement Annuities

- *Foreign Service* — Under both the Foreign Service Retirement and Disability System (FSRDS), covering employees who began service before January 1, 1984, payments of retirement annuities to former spouses *terminate upon remarriage* of the former spouse before age 55 if the remarriage occurred on or after November 8, 1984, or before age 60 if the remarriage occurred prior to November 8, 1984. Under the Foreign Service Pension System (FSPS), covering employees who began service after January 1, 1984, payments of retirement annuities to former spouses end upon remarriage of the former spouse before age 55. FSRDS, 22 U.S.C. §4068; FSPS, 22 U.S.C. §4071j(a)(1)(B).

- *Central Intelligence Agency* — Annuities payable to former spouses are *terminated upon remarriage* of the former spouse before age 55. 50 U.S.C. §403 note, §224, Central Intelligence Agency Retirement Act of 1964 for Certain Employees.

Survivor Benefits

- *Military* — Under the Survivor Benefit Plan applicable to all military members, annuities to widows, widowers or former spouses *terminate if the recipient remarries before age 55.* Payments may resume if the remarriage ends by death, divorce or annulment. However, if the recipient is also entitled to an annuity under the terminated remarriage, he or she must elect which one to receive. 10 U.S.C. §1450(b).

- *Veterans Benefits* — Under Title 38 of the U.S. Code, for purposes of payment of retired pay to surviving spouses and dependency and indemnity compensation, a "surviving spouse" is defined as one who has *not remarried.* 38 U.S.C. §101.

- *Civil Service* — Under both the Civil Service Retirement System (CSRS), covering employees who began service before January 1, 1984, and the Federal Employees' Retirement system (FERS), covering federal employees who began service after January 1, 1984, survivor benefits to former spouses are *terminated upon remarriage before age 55.* CSRS, 5 U.S.C. §8341(h)(3)(B); FERS, 5 U.S.C.§8445(c)(2).

- *Social Security* — Under the Social Security system, benefits for former spouses *terminate upon remarriage of the former spouse.* 42 U.S.C.§402(b)(1)(H) and (c)(1)(H).

Abused Spouses

- Section (h) of 10 U.S.C. §1408, USFSPA, added in 1992, provides that the spouse or former spouse is eligible to receive payments of the retired pay of a military member whose entitlement to retired pay is terminated as a result of misconduct by a member involving abuse of a spouse or dependent child. Payments are made by the government and *continue so long as the former spouse remains unmarried.* This means that, within the same Act, a dichotomy exists in that payments (made by the government) to an abused spouse cease upon remarriage, while payments (made by the military member) to an ex-spouse who was not abused survive remarriage. *This inconsistency (and clear case of discrimination against the military member) begs for resolution.*

Customary Notions of Spousal Support

- Continuation of payments beyond remarriage of former spouses overrides any aspect of financial need. Usually, remarried former spouses attain financial security by virtue of (1) the income of their new marriage partner, or (2) the combination of their own income and that of the new marriage partner. By contrast, a large majority of retired military members whose pay has been divided need to support second families. The inequitable result is that a remarried retired member, most often in great need of his or her retired pay, must continue making payments to a remarried former spouse, who generally no longer needs those payments for financial security.

- As currently written, the USFSPA is inconsistent with customary notions of spousal support in U.S. domestic relations law. An obligation to pay alimony as support for a former spouse generally ceases upon remarriage of the former spouse. This has been standard legal doctrine since the founding of this country, based on the rationale that in a remarriage there is a transfer of spousal support responsibility to the new spouse.

Multiple Payments

- Currently under the USFSPA, a former spouse can acquire more than one award of retired pay by divorcing after a remarriage and remarrying again. Not only is this unfair to the retired member(s) whose pay is being divided on behalf of that former spouse, but it is a situation that encourages divorce. Such cases are not uncommon.

Controversy #10 — Separation Bonuses

A new controversy hit the scene as a result of defense downsizing. The issue revolves around the bonuses service members can get when they agree to cut their careers short in exchange for the lump-sum Special Separation Benefit (SSB) or the Voluntary Separation Incentive (VSI) annuity. These separation payments are in lieu of retirement; thus, a service member forfeits the right to retired pay.

Obviously, if the divorce has already occurred while on active duty, and a portion of the retired pay was awarded prospectively to the former spouse, then the court order to divide retired pay as part of a divorce settlement becomes worthless to the ex-spouse if the military member opts for an early out.

Currently, there is no law or provision in the USFSPA that precludes a court from awarding a former spouse a portion of the separation bonus. However, legislation has been introduced by Rep. Schroeder that would allow state courts to divide, *as property*, monies received by military members as separation bonuses or incentives (see Chapter 12 for more details). Only a few states currently consider severance pay to be marital property.

The subject of separation bonuses could potentially become another legislative tug-of-war, not different from the controversy of the "income vs. property" label put on retired pay. One of the most obvious areas is the potential for accusing the military member of intentionally evading compliance with a divorce decree that orders the member to pay the former spouse a share of the retired pay. Unfortunately, many members must make some very difficult decisions on whether to take the bonus and leave, or face the possibility that another promotion passover or congressional downsizing action may put them out on the street with no bonus whatsoever. Periodically, the various military *Times* publications have published a listing of career fields and statistics on whether the field is expanding or contracting, and the chances of reaching field grade rank or senior enlisted status.

The separation bonus, just like other assets acquired during the marriage, is subject to the domestic family laws of each state. As such, there should be no need for Congress to pass new legislation when judges now have the authority to divide such an asset according to the state law. The military member's concern should be the potential for having to defend his or her decision to leave active duty prior to completing the mandatory years for retirement, and not merely avoiding or appearing to avoid USFSPA payments to the ex-spouse.

Controversy #11 — No Statute of Limitations

Under the law as currently written, there is *no* limitation on the time during which former spouses may seek a share of a member's retired pay. Therefore, divorced military members who may be subject to a claim under the USFSPA must live under a shadow of uncertainty about their retired pay during the lifetime of their former spouse. Not only is this unfair to retired members, but it is inconsistent with common legal practice. Almost every legal action, civil or criminal, has a statutory time beyond which the action may not be brought. Moreover, a statute of limitations *is* provided under other federal retirement systems:

1. *Foreign Service* — To be recognized as valid under the Foreign Service Retirement and Disability System (FSRDS), a court order directing payment of an annuity to a former spouse must be issued within *24 months* of the date of the final divorce. 22 U.S.C. §4054(a)(4).

2. *Central Intelligence Agency* — Court orders for payments from a retirement fund to former spouses must be issued *12 months* after the divorce becomes final. 50 U.S.C. §403 note, Section 222(a)(7). Central Intelligence Agency Retirement Act of 1964 for Certain Employees.

CHAPTER ENDNOTES

1. Letter, dated March 20, 1990, to the Executive Director, American Retirees Association, from Lawrence J. Korb, Director of the Center for Public Policy Education, The Brookings Institution. While serving in the Pentagon during the Reagan admin-

istration, Korb was one of the key framers of the Department of Defense position on USFSPA.

2. The Lambert Gonzales case (*Gonzales v. Roybal*, Civ. No. 93-1302MV, U.S.D.C.N.M.) is currently on appeal with the U.S. District Court for the District of New Mexico. Gonzales petitioned New Mexico's Second Judicial District Court, Bernalillo County, to terminate USFSPA payments on the basis of the 1990 congressional amendment. On June 29, 1993, the court ruled against Master Sergeant Gonzales, reasoning that, under New Mexico law, there is a "limited reservation of jurisdiction" that is incorporated into every NM divorce decree. Under this rationale, the court has ruled that the conditions of the congressional amendment did not apply—and can never apply—in New Mexico. The decision flies in the face of the intent of Congress and is in direct violation of federal law.

3. This computation could be considered the "default" method, in accordance with the literal reading of 10 U.S.C. §1408. Of course, the court can also specify a different amount and method. Thus, each person's final decree may differ.

4. On May 30, 1989, the U.S. Supreme Court in a 7-2 decision ruled that a veteran's disability benefits were not subject to property division in a divorce proceeding. The case stemmed from the 1979 California divorce of retired Air Force Major Gerald Mansell and his wife, Gaye. (Mansell's request in 1983 to modify the divorce decree to exclude disability pay was rejected.) One should note that this ruling does not preclude a court from ordering the member to pay a portion of the retirement pay award from other available income. 109 S.Ct. 2023 (1989), 104 L.Ed.2d 675 (1989), 57 U.S.L.W. 4567, 10 E.B.C. 2521. On remand *In re Marriage of Mansell* (1989, 5th Dist) 216 Cal.App.3d 937, 265 Cal.Rptr. 227, 1989 Cal.App; 217 Cal.App.3d 319, 1989 Ca.App. (Prior history: 487 U.S. 1217, 101 L.Ed.2d 904, 108 S.Ct. 2868).

5. See Chapter 6 for a discussion of the impact of USFSPA on female military members.

6. Effective January 1992, the amount of combined pay a retiree drawing both military retired pay and a Civil Service salary can receive is limited to level V of the executive schedule. This amount exceeded $105,000 in 1993. The exempt amount of dual compensation varies, and is different for those who first became members of a uniformed service before August 1, 1986, and those who first became a member on or after that date.

5

IS IT INCOME
OR IS IT PROPERTY?

While there are a number of continuing controversies surrounding USFSPA, as pointed out in the previous chapter (some of which will probably never get resolved), there is one controversy that has gotten more attention than most.

Truth and Consequences

Inarguably, the most controversial feature of the USFSPA is its reclassification of "pay" as "property." The law, 10 U.S.C. §1408(c)(1) states: "Subject to the limitations of this section, a court may treat disposable **retired pay** payable to a member for pay periods beginning June 25, 1981, either as *property* solely of the member or as **property** of the member and his spouse in accordance with the law of the jurisdiction of such court." (bold type provided)

While postulating that the principal purpose of Congress, in enacting the USFSPA, was to remove the "fence" around military retirement pay placed there by *McCarty*, it is also reasonable to surmise that only a handful of legislators appreciated the full implications of the "property" treatment. Foremost among these is that an award of property under the USFSPA survives the remarriage of the benefitting ex-spouse. This is inconsistent with customary notions of support in U.S. domestic relations law.

It should be noted that Congress could have removed the "*McCarty* fence" around military retired pay simply by legislating that it *could* be used as a source of alimony and child support in a divorce proceeding, but as **pay**, not property. Military veterans may well wonder whether the underlying motivations were vindictiveness and greed, not equity and need—particularly since the USFSPA does not preclude contemporaneous awards of alimony, child support, USFSPA payments, and other assets of the marriage. The astounding result is that state courts are arbitrarily classifying military retirement income as "pay" for some purposes and "property" for others.

The Legal Morass

Divorced military retirees comprise the only class of U.S. citizens who have their income classified, by federal statute, as *both* pay and property. It is believed by many military retirees that this dichotomy derives principally from the response of an inconsistent Congress to the strident demands of feminist pressure groups and the incessant search for "political correctness."

The USFSPA circumvented, but did not supersede, *McCarty*. Congress attempted to imply that it did by taking the unprecedented step of **backdating**[1] the USFSPA to one day prior to *McCarty*. Nevertheless, the core of the *McCarty* ruling (namely, the military retirement system confers no entitlement to retired pay upon retired members' spouses and does not embody even a limited community property concept) still stands. Corroborating evidence of this has been provided by the USFSPA's principal congressional sponsor who regularly introduces legislation to provide an automatic, statutory entitlement to military retirement pay to anyone who marries a military member, from the wedding date onward.

The USFSPA abetted the public misconception of retirement pay as a pension, despite the fact that federal statutes and case law have historically and consistently regarded military retired pay as *reduced compensation for reduced services* with no attributes of a pension. This position has been taken by the Comptroller General, the Defense Department, the Internal Revenue Service, and the U.S. bankruptcy courts. A serious (and, possibly, litigious) anomaly exists in that divorced military members and their ex-spouses are required to pay federal and state *income* taxes on **pay** legally reclassified, by the USFSPA, as **property**.

Legal and Other Precedents

Notwithstanding the fact that Congress can do anything it likes (albeit, subject to Supreme Court review), the following are citations of legal and other precedents that further fuel the "income vs. property" issue.

1. Since the USFSPA was not grandfathered, its effect was to retroactively change the military retirement compensation system. Military members already retired, or eligible for retirement, were caught unexpectedly by a law which they had no reason to anticipate. The failure to grandfather was a failure to provide equal protection under the law for a group

of blindsided American citizens (divorced military veterans) whose lives in retirement were devastated without prior notice and with no compensatory relief. It can be argued that the USFSPA does, in fact, constitute "unjust taking" in violation of protections provided by the Fifth Amendment of the U.S. Constitution.

2. The Armed Forces Voluntary Recruitment Act of 1945 (Public Law 79-190), Section 4, states: "Whenever any enlisted man of the Regular Army shall have completed not less than twenty or more than twenty-nine years of active service, he may upon his own request, *be transferred* to the Enlisted Reserve Corps. An enlisted man so transferred and retired shall receive, except with respect to periods of active duty **he may be required to perform**, until his **death, annual pay**." [bold type added] There is like status for officer personnel. This law clearly defines military pay as wages. If pay is taxed as wages, how, then, can it be property?

3. Retirees have no rights to benefits not yet paid. A lawsuit brought by the National Association of Retired Federal Employees (NARFE) contended that a 3.1 percent COLA became a vested entitlement on December 1, 1985, and, therefore, its cancellation by Gramm-Rudman-Hollings (The Balanced Budget and Emergency Deficit Control Act of 1985) on December 12, 1985, made it illegal. A federal three-judge panel ruled that retirees have no property rights to benefits not yet paid. This was, essentially, upheld by the U.S. Supreme Court by its refusal to hear the appeal.[2]

4. A military retiree's position is unique, in that the military retiree is subject to both civil law *and* the UCMJ, for the remainder of his or her retirement. No other U.S. wage earner is subject to such a commitment as a prerequisite for continued compensation. The elements of a lifetime agreement with the government for continuing reduced pay for reduced services, as defined in *McCarty*, are present and obvious.

5. Article 1, Section 9 of the Constitution specifically states, "No Bill of Attainder or *Ex Post Facto* Law will be passed . . ." Section 10 states that Congress may not "Pass any Bill of Attainder, *ex post facto* law, or Law impairing the obligation of Contracts . . ." (emphasis added) The Fourteenth Amendment reinforces those sections by stating, in part, "nor shall any state deprive any person of life, liberty, or property, without due process of law; nor deny to any person within its jurisdiction the equal protection of the laws." Whether the agreement began and concluded under a law *or* as an agreement, there can be no difference. When one makes an agreement in good faith and spends time in the execution of that agreement, then the government must honor that agreement. A new Congress must uphold the integrity of the old; otherwise, the continuity of congressional commitments is broken and the word of Congress is worthless. Enactment of the USFSPA by the 97th Congress clearly changed a course set for retired military veterans by earlier Congresses.

6. The U.S. Supreme Court in *Buchanan v. Alexander*, 45 U.S. 20 (1846), ruled that money owed by the United States to the individual service member be-

longs to the Treasury until it is paid to that individual. Essentially, the Supreme Court held that courts *cannot* tell a federal disbursing official what to do since it would defeat the purpose for which Congress appropriated the money. If the specific reason Congress appropriates funds for the retired military member after 20 years of active duty is not as compensation for continuing military obligations, what, then, is its reason? What law provides other reasons? The USFSPA provides that a former spouse may receive military retirement pay directly from a military finance center, without sending the money to the military member first.[3] Clearly, this circumvents pay directly to the individual who earns it.

7. The U.S. Supreme Court in *United States v. Tyler*, 105 U.S. 244 (1881), ruled that when the status of the military member changes from active duty, compensation is continued at reduced rate and the connection of the member to the military is continued, with reduced duties and responsibilities. The USFSPA provides that a former spouse may receive up to 50 percent of the monies the military member is paid for fulfilling continuing obligations to the federal government. This money is paid without any corresponding responsibilities whatsoever on the part of the benefitting ex-spouse, who draws from the same pay envelope.

8. Certain sections of the Internal Revenue Code imply that military retirement qualifies as wages and is considered taxable income. Indeed, retirees must report their retired pay as income and pay tax on it. Although 26 U.S.C. §3401, Chapter 24 (Collection of Income

Tax at Source of Wages), defines "wages" to mean "...all remuneration, including the cash value of all remuneration (including benefits)...," there appears to be no provision in the Code flatly stating that military retirement qualifies as wages and is taxable income.

9. The General Accounting Office, in a letter dated February 23, 1990, to an ARA member, stated:

Dear ——:

This is in response to your letter regarding the use of the term pension when referring to retired pay received from a military service.

This office has always maintained that retired service members receive retired pay rather than pensions because they continued to serve after retirement from active duty. In our letter [decision] B-236084, July 31, 1989, concerning Oliver North's retired pay (copy enclosed), we said that military retired pay constitutes current reduced pay for current reduced services, rather than a pension for past services rendered. We have stated this in our decisions since the first volume of published Comptroller General decisions (see 1 Comp.Gen. 700 (1922)).

Our decisions follow the reasons of the Supreme Court in United States v. Tyler, *105 U.S. 244 (1881), in which the Court said that after a member's retirement, 'compensation is continued at a reduced rate, and the connection [of the member to the military] is continued, with a retirement from active service only.'*

We share your concern that the news media sometimes inaccurately refer to military retired pay as a pension.

10. The term "property" describes one's right to possess, use, and dispose of a thing as well as the object, benefit, or prerogative which constitutes the subject matter of that right. Since it has been ruled that the federal and military retiree has no vested interest in his/her retired pay (it cannot be sold, given away, or passed on to heirs), it fails the test of legal property: that of disposability by its owner. It is subject to the terms of enlistment or employment, and thereafter, the terms of retirement.

11. For any law within the United States to be truly valid, it must, first, meet the requirements of the Constitution and become effective only from its actual date of passage. It cannot be postdated. To be fair, it must also be universally applied, nondiscriminatory, consistent in its application, and equitable in its considerations. The applications of, and the passage of the USFSPA itself, meet *none* of these requirements.

The Bottom Line

If there is a "bottom line" on the *pay vs. property* issue, it is that military retirement pay fails the legal test of property: that of disposability by its owner. Military retirement pay cannot be sold, transferred, or passed on to heirs. Furthermore, the military member is not *vested* in the retirement pay the way a civilian employee is. The member must serve[4] at least 20 years of honorable service.[5]

Surrounding this fundamental failure are a plethora of conflicting and confusing statutes, court decisions and precedents. The legal arena is rich with opportunities for litigation, either to repeal the USFSPA or to amend it to bring it into conformance in the numerous arenas where it is in conflict.

The most notable relevant litigation to date is the "Unjust Taking" case which was ruled on by the U.S. Court of Appeals for the federal circuit on July 16, 1990 (Appendix E). The ruling deftly sidestepped the constitutional (and other) issues involved.

The principal determinants for further litigation are:

- a conviction that it would be successful and have the curative effects desired;
- the legal talent to prepare and successfully argue the case;
- the financial resources to pay for it.

The ball, while clearly in the court of those current USFSPA victims who have the will and the resources to litigate, is also in the court of every military member who wishes to preserve the constitutional principles underlying retired pay (notwithstanding fair divisions of marital assets in a divorce action). Little, if any, help can be expected from any other members of the national community of veterans' organizations because they consider other veterans' issues more important than repeal or reform of the USFSPA.

In the meantime, USFSPA victims must continue to look to Congress to right the wrongs it has wrought with this unbalanced and discriminatory law. For their part, state divorce courts will continue to make the awards of military retired pay—as property—the USFSPA empowers them to make.

CHAPTER ENDNOTES

1. Mike Causey, who writes "The Federal Diary" column in *The Washington Post*, said it best in his feature titled, "Give and Take on Benefits" (May 10, 1993, p. D2), in response to those who contend "Congress *cannot* change the system because it wouldn't be fair or right" [in reference to lowering survivor benefits for federal retirees]. He goes on to say: "Let's go back to Civics 101. Congress can do most anything it wants. It changes laws and rules all the time....Just because a proposed change may be wrong, or unpopular, doesn't mean it can't happen. Citizens are entitled to fight for or against changes. But they are wrong when they say Congress *cannot* [Causey's emphasis] do something."

2. Source: *Air Force Times*, January 12, 1987.

3. For the spouse to receive *direct* payment from the military finance center, the marriage has to have lasted at least 10 years during which the military member performed 10 years of creditable service.

4. Spouses, however, become entitled to a direct payment of a share of the member's retirement pay after only **10** years, according to the USFSPA. See Chapter 6 for a discussion of this anomaly of female military members married to other members.

5. Recent changes related to the Defense Department downsizing have resulted in an early retirement offer, which comes with many restrictions. (There are also exceptions for members who are medically retired.)

6

WOMEN
IN UNIFORM

When the USFSPA was first introduced into Congress, early debates centered on the "plight of the military wife" and recognized her important contributions to military life in deference to her husband's career and to the detriment of her own. And, although USFSPA is gender neutral—it applies to all people in uniform, both men and women —the concern was not, as the testimony clearly points out, for the civilian male with a military *wife*.[1] In fact, the only pronoun appearing in the USFSPA itself in connection with military retirement pay is "his."

There are approximately 1,106,600 female military veterans in the United States. This is exclusive of the number of women currently on active duty and in the National Guard, Reserves, and Coast Guard. It is only recently that female married military members are beginning to be affected by the USFSPA, as the percentage of women entering the armed forces and staying in for a career increases.

Female Military Must Get in Line Behind the Non-Military Wife

It is the female military member, however, who must get in line behind a nonmilitary wife. Perhaps the anomaly of this situation can best be summed up in the words of ARA member Major (then Captain) Kimberly K. Power, MSC, who wrote in a letter to Congress:[2]

> *Under USFSPA MY CONTRIBUTION TO THIS NATION'S SECURITY IS FAR MORE VALUABLE IN MY ROLE AS MILITARY WIFE THAN IN MY ROLE AS A MILITARY OFFICER [capitalization by letter's author]. According to USFSPA, I am vested in 15 years' worth of my husband's retirement benefits [having been married for that length of time currently], yet after my ten years of service I have no entitlements to my own retirement. I must serve a full 20 years to receive anything based on my own military career. The lack of logic and fairness is mind boggling.*

DACOWITS

The civilian organization known as the Defense Advisory Committee on Women in the Service (DACOWITS) has, as its charter, the responsibility to address the needs and welfare of women in the military. It meets at least twice a year. For two years running, Major Power was instrumental in bringing the USFSPA issue to the attention of DACOWITS as it relates to women military members.

The thrust of Major Power's address to the DACOWITS on April 24, 1991, at its spring conference, was that it was "high time the DACOWITS treat the concerns of military women as being of higher priority than the interests of civilians previously married to military personnel." From the perspective of national security, certainly there can be no argument that the contributions of women in uniform far surpass those of most women in mufti.

To date, DACOWITS has refused to take a stand supporting military women on this legislation, despite the fact that USFSPA has been the biggest blow to women in the military in many years, "outranked," perhaps, only by the women in combat issue. Perhaps if one of the criteria for being on the committee were prior military service, the USFSPA issue would get the attention it deserves.

Times Have Changed

If you were to read the original testimony of the hearings held before Congress in 1982, you would find that the typical civilian spouse of a military member was portrayed as a non-working wife who devoted her full time to her husband and family and needed lifetime support because she was incapable of working.

This concept is inconsistent with the social and economic realities of the 1990s. Given the constantly growing presence of women in the workplace and their contributions to society as a whole (not just to the military family), the "plight of the military spouse," as advertised during Congress' 1982 pro-USFSPA debate/discussion, may no longer be valid, if it ever was.

Today's military spouse is a "working" spouse. Indeed, the number of working military spouses now exceeds 60 percent of the present population.

Career Discrimination

Many women in uniform who are informed on this

issue feel this law obstructs the careers of America's military women and deprives them of earned entitlements. In the words of Major Power, "We have worked too hard for the gains made to allow any law to discourage our female officers and NCOs from seeking full and rewarding careers."[3]

As more women join the armed forces, this issue may take on new importance as more and more *men* are added to the ranks of USFSPA beneficiaries.

CHAPTER ENDNOTES

1. Were the situation reversed, we find it hard to think that Congress would have been so sympathetic toward the male who would give up his career to be the "backbone of the military family."

2. Letter, dated May 14, 1991, to the Honorable Beverly B. Byron, then chairperson of the House Armed Services Subcommittee on Military Personnel and Compensation.

3. See endnote #2 above.

THE RESERVES AND
THE GUARD

As you will read in Chapter 8, there are several issues that are unique to a military divorce which can make the process much more difficult than a divorce between civilians. Adding to the complications are the military member's status if he or she is a reservist.

When the military member is a reservist, the information available on calculations of the retiree's pay for the former spouse is much scarcer, if not totally lacking. The issue has not really been addressed at all. Two other important issues—calculation of the length of marriage versus the reservist's "good years" for retirement purposes and the matter of nonpay for reserve duty—have not been addressed adequately, if at all.

A reservist is eligible to draw retired pay upon reaching age 60 and after completing at least 20 years of qualifying military service (commonly referred to as "good" years), the last eight of which were served as a member of a reserve component (this applies to former active duty members who become reservists or join the National Guard). It is important to understand that certain kinds of service do not count as qualifying service. For example, the time one spends in the Inactive Reserve does not count as qualifying service. In another example, insufficient retirement points, even for creditable service, may not have been earned in a given year.

Besides completing a "good year" for retirement purposes, the reservist must also complete fiscal year training requirements. The two time-frames are usually not the same. 10 U.S.C. §1331 (1956) established a new principle governing the retirement of reservists. It was codified in August 1956, and has its legal authority in Chapter 67, Title 10, United States Code, sections 1331-1337. (Reserve retirement is commonly referred to as Title III.)

Reservists Are Not Always Compensated with Money

The active duty person earns money for every day of active duty. Both the active duty time (which is usually consecutive) and the pay earned are considered in divorce settlements. The reservist, on the other hand, may be in a nonpay category or status and still be required to put in the time (i.e., work).

It could be argued, then, that it is the reservist's efforts and not the "community's efforts" that are involved. Yet, the military reservist's retired pay would be divided on the basis of the law and not on the merits of the peculiarities associated with reserve duty. While most reserve duty is performed on the weekend, many reservists also perform their duty during the week by taking personal leave from their own jobs. Others put in extra time in the evenings.

Does the "Plight" Apply to Spouses of Reservists?

Is there a "hardship" for the spouse in such cases? Indeed, the hardship is the burden of the reservist—working outside the normal job and, often, for no pay! Yet, in a divorce, the reservist's retirement pay upon reaching age 60 would be subject to division.

Legal Literature Lacking

Whether the USFSPA applies to reservists is addressed in detail in an article written by Captain Karen A. MacIntyre in 1983.[1] Despite the date of this article, the logic of the information is, for the most part, still relevant.

The point to be made here is that the "hardships" and inequities that were originally cited as the main reasons for changing the law do not exist when the military member is a reservist. Captain MacIntyre has examined in detail the "language" of the original statute to determine whether reservists were ever meant to fall under this law. (The article does not, however, address the issue of a "good year" in accounting for the time on which the reservist's eventual retirement pay will be based. In the case of the reservist, it may take more than one year to accumulate enough "points" to equal "one good year" for retirement purposes.)

To understand the problems in calculating the share of retired pay that will go to the ex-spouse, look at the following example.

A reservist, age 50, married 12 years, has just completed "20 good years" for retirement purposes. But it actually took him 24 years to get "20 years that counted." He won't begin (by law), however, to draw retired pay until age 60. The entire time he has been married he has been a reservist. He divorces at age 55. How is the retired pay awarded the spouse calculated? Is it based on one-half of 20 years' retirement? 24 years?[2]

As more and more active duty military leave the service and join the reserves, this issue may take on new importance in the near future.

Bottom Line for Reservists—You Are Subject to the USFSPA

Members of the Reserve and National Guard **are** subject to the mandates of the USFSPA. And, if you qualify for retired pay and are divorced, your ex-spouse could be awarded up to 50 percent of it.

CHAPTER ENDNOTES

1. Captain Karen A. MacIntyre. *A Legal Assistance Symposium—Division of U.S. Army Reserve and National Guard Pay Upon Divorce*. 102 Mil.L.Rev. 232 (Fall 1983).

2. Some states would calculate the share to the ex-spouse on the basis of the number of points (a percentage thereof) earned during the period of the marriage that also fell during the period of active reserve duty. As already pointed out, this method of calculation does not consider that some of the points may have been earned in a nonpay status.

8

ALL DIVORCES ARE NOT ALIKE: WHAT YOU NEED TO CONSIDER

This chapter, indeed, this book, is not meant to be a treatise on domestic relations law. The military member needs to be aware, however, of the many issues that can affect his or her divorce.

"Military" Divorce vs. "Civilian" Divorce

Military divorces are, in many respects, no different from other (civilian) divorces. While one might argue that military couples are faced with more and greater hardships than the average civilian couple, making it difficult to maintain a marriage and family life, military divorce will, nevertheless, involve procedural requirements, property distribution, and perhaps child support or maintenance. It is the problem of the division of military retirement pay, the basis for this book, that presents some unusual considerations in military divorces.

Issues Unique to a Military Divorce

There are numerous issues that are unique to a military divorce which can render the process much more difficult than a civilian divorce. They include:

1. Status of the military member at the time of divorce: active duty, reserve, retired.
2. Pay grade of military member at time of divorce.
3. Divorce that is initiated when one or both spouses are overseas.
4. Previous military divorce.
5. Direct payment versus an allotment for payment to ex-spouse.
6. Entitlement of military member to disability pay.
7. Disposable vs. gross retired pay (for calculation purposes).
8. Type of discharge from the service.
9. Domicile issue (for jurisdiction purposes).
10. Due process requirements for the military member and the Soldiers' and Sailors' Civil Relief Act of 1940.
11. Pre- and post-retirement employment (and dual compensation restriction).
12. Length of marriage during the military career as a determinant for receiving military benefits (such as medical care, commissary and exchange privileges).
13. Status of military member after divorce (active duty, already retired, disabled retiree, reservist, dual compensation in case where retiree returns to work for the federal government)—officer, enlisted, regular, or reserve.

14. Survivor Benefit Plan for former or current spouse.
15. Military member as single parent (custody of children).
16. Conversion of military retirement time with subsequent Civil Service employment (to receive a Civil Service pension).
17. Treatment of separation bonuses (SSB and VSI) in a divorce proceeding.
18. Treatment of abused military spouses.

Military Benefits an Important Consideration

Members of the military and their families are entitled to numerous benefits. Depending on the length of the marriage, military spouses may also be entitled to benefits based on the retirement status of their marital partners. Minor children's entitlements are not affected by the divorce. We have chosen to address these benefits because they can become part of the predivorce negotiations and, indeed, in many cases, should be addressed in the divorce decree (e.g., whether or what portion of the retirement remains the military member's, and what share goes to the former spouse; whether the military member retains the choice of beneficiary for SBP).

The benefits that may be extended to the former spouse include commissary, exchange, and medical. Based on the length of the marriage, combined with the military member's active duty time, the ex-spouse may be entitled to continue receiving these benefits. In fact, it may be in the military member's best interests, if very close to the 20-year point, to remain married in order for the spouse to receive all the benefits he or she is currently receiving. Given that some military families do not amass any extensive list of assets or retirement vehicles (stocks, bonds, etc.), the military benefits may end up being the major assets that an ex-spouse receives. As the saying goes, "Timing is everything."

20/20/20 and 20/20/15 Spouses

The term 20/20/20 is one that you will see often in any discussion of USFSPA. A former spouse may qualify for certain benefits and privileges, depending on the length of the marriage, the number of years of military service creditable for retired pay, and the overlap of marriage and military service. To qualify for all benefits at the time of divorce, an unremarried former spouse must have been married for at least 20 years to a military member who performed at least 20 years of service creditable for retired pay, and there must also have been a 20-year overlap of marriage and military service (20/20/20). A 20/20/15 spouse is one where there was an overlap of at least 15 years.

If a former spouse is covered by an employer-sponsored health plan, medical care is not authorized (medical care may be reinstated when the former spouse is no longer covered by an employer-sponsored health plan). A former spouse who qualifies for 20/20/20, who lost eligibility because of remarriage, and who subsequently became unmarried through divorce or death of the spouse, is entitled to reinstatement of commissary, base exchange, and theater privileges only. No medical care is authorized (Public Laws 97-252, 98-525, and 100-565). There are other rules governing a 20/20/15 marriage where the divorce occurred before April 1, 1985, or on or after September 30, 1988.

There have been continuing attempts to provide PX/BX and commissary privileges to ex-spouses who do not meet the 20/20/20 or 20/20/15 criteria. If shopping privileges are an issue in your divorce, you should contact the

American Retirees Association to ascertain the status of current legislative activity in this arena.

The Abused Military Dependents Act

If you are charged with domestic violence under the Abused Military Dependents Act (AMDA) of 1992,[1] you could lose your retirement altogether, but your dependents may not. The AMDA requires the military services to pay an annuity, based on the retirement pay to which a military member may have lost entitlement by reason of abuse of dependents, to eligible spouses and former spouses.

Eligibility ceases if the benefitting ex-spouse remarries. The original (draft) legislation provided for the loss of benefits if the abused spouse resumed cohabitation with the abuser. Since this was not retained in the amendment as enacted, it must be presumed that an abused spouse may continue to receive payments of retirement pay if she does not divorce and remarry—or, in short, resumes cohabitation with her abuser.

Notwithstanding the obligation and need to support the military dependents when such abuse cases arise, here we have, in the same section of Title 10 of the U.S. Code, conflicting provisions on the remarriage of ex-spouses receiving military retirement pay. It is worth noting also that the AMDA, when it originated in the Senate, included a statute of limitations provision which was eliminated in the subsequent House-Senate conference committee. This is yet another example of the sloppy legal work which has characterized the crafting of the USFSPA since its inception in 1982, and is discussed in more detail in Chapter 12.

Dependent Support

Another area that can cause trouble is that of dependent support. Again, it is not worth the possibility of extended litigation (where the court takes matters into its own hands) to get in trouble over basic entitlements or privileges. The military expects its members to support their dependents and, based on marital status, gives them extra money to do so. For example, if the military member is receiving a housing allowance at the "with dependents" rate, based on the status of being married, then it would be foolish to withhold that housing allowance from the spouse. To do so could be considered a change in status—if dependents are not receiving the allowance, then the military member does not need it.

It is **illegal** for a military member to refuse to support his dependents while receiving allowances at the "with dependents" rate. Refusing to do so could result in any number of actions, not the least of which is a court-martial and a discharge! Further, if there is a court order to pay support, the dependents could have the military member's pay (active duty, reserve, or retired) garnished.

Child custody can be complicated, since a dilemma is posed between what is best for the child (e.g., the military member is the one entitled to the benefits) and how the military member will be able to fulfill all of his or her military obligations. The member is required to have a guardian for the children so the member is free to be sent worldwide without notice for national security purposes.

Married members and those with dependents actually do receive more money just for having a spouse or dependents. Single members do not share in additional funds.

SBP—Don't Ignore The Preretirement Notification Requirements

Approximately 90 days prior to retirement, active duty members are briefed on the Survivor Benefit Plan. Military members will have the choices of declining it, accepting it with full base coverage (see The Retired Officers Association's publication on SBP, Appendix N), or accepting it with some other amount of base coverage. *If the military member declines SBP or accepts less than full base coverage, the spouse must concur in writing.* The fact that a military member might be undergoing a divorce does not relieve the services of their legal obligation to notify the spouse. If the military member refuses to let them notify his or her spouse, and the spouse does not agree with the choice, the law says that the military member will be enrolled at the maximum amount (for which a 6.5% premium is deducted from the gross retired pay). The survivor receives 55 percent of the selected base amount of the member's retired pay.

How does this affect divorcing members? The problem occurs when the couple goes to negotiate the terms of the divorce settlement. If the court ends up ordering the military member to carry SBP on the spouse and the member must pay the premium, then that premium could be for the *full* base coverage if the spouse has not concurred.

Example

Assume retired pay is $2500 a month. The monthly SBP premium will be $162.50 (the military member gets a tax break, however, as it is deducted before taxes are figured). Moreover, whatever the member does pay as SBP premiums for an ex-spouse may be deducted from the amount of the USFSPA payments due the spouse.

Let's now say that the military member had consulted the spouse and she might have agreed to a less-than-full base coverage amount of $1000 (she would receive $550 per month upon the member's death). The premium would then be only $65 each month. However, since the law only allows the military member to use the amount in effect at the time of retirement (in this case, the member refused to process the paperwork), the military member would be required to elect full base coverage. It may be possible *to increase the coverage during open season,* when there is one, but it cannot be decreased, once it is selected.

Thus, it would behoove the member to (1) not ignore the paperwork just because he might be angry with his spouse; and (2) discuss the matter with his spouse or through her attorney, *before* he officially retires.

The decision to act promptly and maturely in this matter could save the military member a lot of money. Failure to act prudently might also mean that the court might order the military member to pay the premium.

It is very important, then, that the military member understand the requirements of SBP and consult with the spouse or through the spouse's attorney. Remember, SBP may be an important element of any predivorce negotiations. It is a very valuable asset which could offered in exchange for other considerations during a divorce settlement.

Social Security

Although not exclusively a military benefit, social security may figure importantly in a military divorce action. The ex-spouse of a member is entitled to the same benefits he or she would get if still married to the member, which is a sum equal to half of the member's check if the member is still alive, or to the full amount if the member has died, *provided that*:

1. The couple was married at least 10 years.
2. The ex-spouse is not currently married.
3. The ex-spouse did not earn enough on the job to be eligible for a benefit equal to or greater than their military spouse's.
4. The military member has filed for social security benefits, or else the ex-spouse is over age 62 and has been divorced for more than two years. (The 2-year waiting period is waived if the military member was entitled to social security benefits before the divorce.)

The ex-spouse's benefit does not affect that of the military member. Similarly, if the military member remarries, the subsequent spouse's benefits do not affect those of the divorced ex-spouse. If the ex-spouse remarries, he or she can choose whether to apply on the account of the former or current marital partner.

With all the hue and cry about "the plight of the military spouse," social security benefits are frequently overlooked in calculating what an ex-spouse will receive, thus bolstering claims to USFSPA payments, child support, other marital assets, and whatever else may be assessed and divided from a session in divorce court.

Jurisdiction

The issue of jurisdiction in a divorce is also complicated, since meeting residency requirements and notifying the other spouse may present severe problems. Frequent moves may mean that not enough time has transpired for the servicemember to be considered a resident. The usual proof for establishing residency is often lacking, such as length of residency, owning a home, paying taxes in the state, voting, etc. Some states may, however, have special requirements that allow service members to get divorces even though they are not legal residents in the traditional sense of the word.

In most divorces, property is divided. In a military marriage, this often may not include a house, or even substantial financial assets. The military member's retirement benefits may be the only asset worth dividing.

Timing Can Work to Both the Military Member's and Spouse's Advantage

The uniqueness of the military, thus, presents some interesting, if not unusual, considerations in divorces, particularly in the areas of general benefits, child custody, jurisdiction for filing purposes, and retirement pay. It may be more advantageous for the military couple to separate rather than divorce for the time being, particularly if the couple is approaching the 20-year point, when the member will become eligible for retirement pay. By doing so, the military spouse remains eligible for military benefits, and some of the major issues usually raised in a contested divorce might be avoided.

Timing becomes even more important when Defense is downsizing its active and reserve forces, and subsequently initiating early-outs (voluntary), and causing involuntary separation or reductions in force (RIFs), and involuntary retirement based on a selective early retirement board (SERBs), and early retirement (the new 15-year retirement eligibility).

Thus, it is even more critical that the military member know that there are issues unique to a military divorce, just as timing in a civilian divorce can be critical to successful financial planning and each party's subsequent share of the marital assets. The list cited at the beginning of this chapter should serve as a checklist of items the military member may need to discuss with an attorney.

Do's and Don't's

The divorce process is bad enough without further complicating it, but sometimes we are our own worst enemies. There are numerous stories about military members who refused to do certain things. For example, if you retire and you and your spouse are separated, the spouse must get a new identification (I.D.) card to reflect your retired status.[2] The member must sign the paperwork for the spouse to get a new I.D. card. Do not refuse to do so.

Likewise, if either party is relocating when the divorce occurs, with the member going to one location and the spouse to another, do not decide that you will refuse to file any loss or damage claims for your spouse's household goods that were (or will be) moved under your orders.

The military member is the sponsor, and the spouse is dependent on the sponsor for a number of things. Some of these things may create problems for you. For example, you may be held liable for costs incurred if your ex-spouse is hospitalized in a military facility because you will be identified on his or her ID card (now) as the sponsor, along with your social security number. It will require time and, perhaps, money to extricate yourself.

Refusing to comply with entitlements that are due the spouse only aggravates an already difficult situation. Needless to say, you don't look very good in the eyes of your base personnel or finance center either, not to mention your commander. In fact, you could appear rather immature and petty. Members are only hurting themselves when they fail to carry through with regular actions that are expected of them.

Compliance with the Law Is in Your Best Interests

One last comment is in order. Do not withhold any support and do not refuse to execute all paperwork for the entitlements which your dependents would normally receive. To do so is asking for trouble and could jeopardize your divorce settlement. It just plain isn't worth it.

CHAPTER ENDNOTES

1. Public Law 102-484, FY 1993 National Defense Authorization Act. This law has been added as subsection (h) to 10 U.S.C. §1408 (USFSPA).

2. As any military member or spouse knows, your status is a factor in the use and receipt of military privileges and benefits. For example, some bases will not provide medical care to military retirees' dependents because they don't have enough trained personnel or staff. Dependents must seek medical care through the Civilian Health and Medical Program of the Uniformed Services (CHAMPUS).

9

THE DIVORCE PROCESS

What You Need to Know If You Plan to Divorce

This book is not meant to be a procedural guide for divorce, but you do need to know what some of the "military" implications and complications are for some of the routine steps in the initial phases of the divorce process. As a military member, you (as well as your spouse) may be able to go to your local base or post legal office to obtain *general* information on the following for your state: general filing and residency requirements, service, grounds, support (spousal and child), property division, and appeal rights. Keep in mind, however, that your local military legal office[1] may not be able to answer any specific questions, particularly if the military lawyer is not a domestic relations expert. If you do not have a military legal office nearby, then you should educate yourself regarding the following points so that you can maximize your discussions with your chosen attorney (and minimize your legal fees).

General Filing and Residency Requirements

As mentioned in Chapter 8, the issue of jurisdiction in a divorce can be very complicated, since meeting residence requirements and notifying the other spouse may present severe problems, particularly when one is out of the country or serving in combat. Frequent moves may mean that not enough time has passed to be considered a resident. The usual proof for establishing residency may be lacking with a military couple, such as owning a home, paying taxes in the state, voting, etc. Some states may, however, have special requirements that allow service members to get divorces even though they are not legal residents.

Some of the questions that can be raised, then, concerning meeting the general requirements, are: Do you file in the county in which you are a resident or in which your spouse resides? In other words, if you claim one state and your spouse claims another, what are your state's venue requirements? One state might require you to file in the county in which the defendant (your spouse) resides, another in which grounds accrue; or, if the defendant is a nonresident, you might be able to file in any county in the state. Some states require that you be a resident for six months prior to filing for divorce; others require one year.

If you think you may be eligible to file in more than one state, you may wish to select the state which has the simpler procedures. Exercise caution, however, if you are currently living in one location and choose to have your divorce processed in another state. What may start out to be a "no fault" or amicable divorce may end up in litigation. Long-distance calls to and from your attorney will add up fast, not to mention FAX charges and overnight mail. You could even be required to attend more than one hearing or deposition or have to travel to that state for unforeseen court-related requirements. Worse yet, you could be ordered to pay such costs for your spouse. Obviously, in some cases, you will not have a choice as to where the divorce is processed.

If you are still on active duty, claiming residency is further complicated by the fact that you continually move around. Do not get lulled into thinking that just because you claim a certain state on your "Leave and Earnings Statement" (LES), that state will be the one to retain jurisdiction over you for divorce purposes. Although some states are obviously more liberal when it comes to what you need to "prove" that you live there, others are not so lenient. A driver's license alone, the claiming of a state on your LES, or the fact you were previously stationed in a state, will usually not be enough.

One last comment about filing—if divorce is your final decision, then it does not matter whether the husband or the wife files for divorce. The courts do not presume that one is at fault more than another, or that the plaintiff (the one who files first) is "not guilty."

Service—Having Divorce Papers Served

The law states that the other party has the right to be notified of any divorce action and to be given sufficient time to respond. This process is called "service of process," and the other party is said to be "served" or "served papers." These papers are the legal notice of the divorce, and neither party should ignore such service. Each state has its own rules for service, such as how it may be done (e.g., personal delivery by the sheriff, publication, certified mail with return receipt requested), and how many days ahead the service must take place prior to a hearing. In addition, if your nonmilitary spouse serves you with papers while you are on active duty, then there must also be a statement called (the title varies) a Soldiers and Sailors Affidavit.[2,3] This form is a safeguard for the military defendant who does not answer the complaint (e.g., divorce petition) or appear at a hearing. The form is a sworn statement and often has to be signed in the presence of a notary public.

Grounds for Divorce

The choices here are usually no-fault and fault. Within these two categories, there are various other requirements. For example, one state may allow a divorce under no-fault and call it irreconcilable differences, either 90 days after filing the complaint with mutual consent or after a 3-year separation without mutual consent. Another state might also allow no-fault, and require only one year of living apart as part of a separation decree. In still others, the time periods may depend on whether there are minor children.

Be advised here that the wording for the grounds is usually standard (i.e., your state has particular wording to use). You might find the wording in your divorce petition rather old-fashioned or even outrageous or insulting, perhaps stronger than what you would use to describe marital conflict which cannot be resolved. Although you might try asking your attorney to use different wording, do not be surprised to hear that is what is always used.

In addition to no-fault grounds, there are fault grounds. Fault grounds include adultery, extreme cruelty, desertion, habitual drunkenness, felony conviction, permanent insanity, and other situations. Some states have completely abolished fault grounds. Others require an extensive set of rules and procedures to prove the grounds.

If you wish to proceed on the basis of a fault divorce, then you should question your attorney as to his or her experience with that type of divorce. Keep in mind that there will be a lot more paperwork to prove the ground, more court appearances, more delays, and in general, the whole matter will likely take more time than a no-fault divorce.

We need not tell you that your attorney fees will accrue rapidly in a fault-grounds divorce. Indeed, some lawyers charge a flat fee to appear in court for you, whether it takes one hour or one day. And you are usually billed for the time the attorney sits around waiting for a courtroom or a judge, as they have blocked that time for you.

Although it was the intent of the no-fault grounds to remove much of the adversarial nature of divorce, this is not always the case. By its very nature, a divorce is an adversary action. And, while your divorce may end up being uncontested (there is no full-blown trial), it will probably involve a lot of unpleasant meetings, with parties on all sides very angry that the whole process is not moving faster.

We cannot stress enough how important it is that you and your spouse try to resolve all issues out of court. Try formulating a separation agreement before you go to court. There are various books (Nolo Press in California is known for its legal self-help publications, which can be found in bookstores) that can assist you with checklists.

Spousal Support

Support is often called maintenance or alimony. It can be temporary or permanent, or be "reserved" (the party may request it later). In some states, fault is considered in the award of support, in others, it is not. A state may even disallow court-ordered permanent alimony (if that is the case, the parties may be able to agree to periodic payments). Maintenance may also be non-monetary. Sometimes support ends automatically at remarriage or ends with cohabitation. Or, there may be no statutory provisions for termination upon remarriage.

If your state can award permanent alimony, and the court will also award a portion of your retired pay, then it is in your best interests to inform your attorney of both you and your spouse's situations relative to support. The factors the court will consider (as will you and your spouse's attorneys) are your age and health, your potential for supplementary income (in addition to your retired pay) as well as your future earning ability, educational level, standard of living during the marriage, and the length of your marriage, among other considerations. Do not overlook the fact that your spouse may qualify for various military benefits, such as medical and commissary. If you both cannot agree on the amount or type of support, then be prepared for the courts to decide for you. Like child support, some courts have schedules that the judges can use, based on income.

Child Support

Child support varies from state to state. Most states now have charts or schedules where the courts do not even have to "think" this issue through—the charts state how much support will be awarded based on number of children and income. (You can usually get a sample child support schedule from the court clerk, or look up the schedule in the "Family" or "Domestic Relations" portion of your state's code.) A state may require that a bond be posted. In some states mandatory wage assignment is made. Generally, the award of child support can be modified based on changed circumstances (although other provisions of the divorce decree cannot).

Keep in mind here that the award of either maintenance or child support or both can be *in addition* to the award of retired pay. Although the military finance center will not pay out more than 65 percent (50 percent for division of property, plus 15 percent for child support) of the retiree's pay directly to the former spouse, this does not mean that the court cannot award more than that amount. The difference will have to come directly from the pocket of the military member.

We empathize with those members whose retired pay is their only source of income. But keep in mind that the duty to support children is paramount in the court's view, as well as society's, and it is your responsibility and legal duty to provide support. It is also your responsibility, as mentioned earlier, to keep your attorney informed. This means providing your attorney with a listing of your monthly living expenses, an inventory of your property, and some kind of forecast as to your current and future financial requirements.

Property Division

Property can be tangible (e.g., a house) and intangible (e.g., professional license), and is distributed in one of three ways—equitable distribution, community property, and common law title. Sometimes fault is considered in the award of property. Many states now recognize the contribution of the nonworking spouse and include the economic value of the homemaker's contribution as a marital asset.

Although most states recognize the homemaker's nonmonetary contribution, keep in mind that the USFSPA does not require a showing of the military spouse's contributions in order for the court to award a share of the retired pay. In other words, unlike civilian divorces where property division is often based on financial and economic need and a host of other considerations, the military spouse need not prove anything other than the length of the marriage in order to receive a portion of the military retirement pay. (Congressional testimony during the time that USFSPA was being considered does contain comments relative to the "plight" of the military spouse.)

It can be argued that in the 1990s, the original intent of USFSPA has changed. Indeed, the trend in state courts is to not award alimony when both spouses are able to support themselves. This has little or nothing to do with a USFSPA award.

Property also includes pensions and retirement benefits, vested and nonvested. Most states determine the right to such property by dividing the number of years the employed spouse was both a member of a retirement plan and married by the number of years of work required before the pension payments will be made. Despite the USFSPA's lack of a provision that computes the award based on number of years of marriage, some states are making the division using such a formula. (ARA's legislative agenda includes equity in this regard.) Keep in mind that the USFSPA requires the marriage to have lasted 10 years (during 10 years of military duty) in order for the former spouse to receive direct payment from the finance center. The marriage can last less time and still qualify for a division of the retired pay.

Of positive note (albeit the true percentage share is reduced) is that if you were divorced before February 5, 1991, then the portion of your retired pay going to a former spouse is based on a net disposable figure (versus the gross amount). What this means to you is that disposable pay is figured after the amounts withheld for income tax, and you can deduct your payments to your former spouse as if they were alimony on your federal income tax return. Caution: Disposable pay for divorces on and after February 5, 1991 is figured pretax.

Appeal Rights

Your divorce is usually not "final" until an appeal period has passed. Most states allow a party to appeal a divorce judgment within 30 days of the entry of the judgment. What this means is that if either party plans to remarry, he or she must wait until the appeal period has ended. Appeals rarely occur in uncontested divorces. If the divorce was contested and you felt that the court was unfair or some action was taken in error, then you have the right to appeal. (If you have selected a competent and thorough attorney, such actions should be unnecessary.)

Do not confuse appeal rights, however, with the fact that you might be dissatisfied with your divorce judgment. If you failed to raise an issue in your original complaint or hearing, then your action (failure to do so) will be construed as a waiver of your right to raise the same issue on appeal. For example, consider the military member who is notified that he or she is being retired early involuntarily (e.g., a SERB action). Perhaps the individual feels he is now being forced to accept a lower standard of living because of not being able to stay in the military longer to earn more money and, hence, a higher retired paycheck. He might overlook telling this to his lawyer. The military member cannot now raise the issue of the SERB action on appeal and how that action has cut short his plans to save more for his retirement years. Keep in mind that disobeying or ignoring court orders can constitute waivers, also.

Careful planning and the selection of a competent lawyer will minimize, if not eliminate, any need for you to appeal. This does not mean that the other party cannot appeal. What it does mean is that you ask your attorney what the appeal waiting period is, and you do not go out and remarry immediately until that time has passed.

Your Base Legal Office

You may be wondering whether to seek advice through your local judge advocate general's office. Most large military installations will have a legal office with one or more "JAGs" and a (senior) staff judge advocate, including civilian lawyers. Although the military attorneys can provide some help with personal legal matters (e.g., they can prepare a will for you free of charge, or review a lease, etc.), the military member and the spouse are responsible for seeking a civilian attorney in divorce matters.

The military attorneys can advise both parties of their rights and benefits, provide checklists and forms for accomplishing a separation agreement, and assist in helping the spouse obtain family support. This assistance will be done only in person and not over the phone. The legal offices will often have literature available pertinent to the state where you are serving in, along with fact sheets on the USFSPA and SBP.

Occasionally you may meet a reservist who is performing an annual two-week active duty tour in the base legal office. And, you may be lucky to learn that the reservist is a practicing attorney (you are really lucky if the attorney/reservist is a domestic relations lawyer!) in the local area (or in the state) who knows the state rules and procedures. Such a resource can be invaluable to you as you begin the process. But, keep in mind that the reservist is there for only a short period, and that it is still your responsibility to retain a civilian attorney.

CHAPTER ENDNOTES

1. Some military legal offices actually do help couples process their divorce. However, in one instance we know of, the civilian lawyer working in the military legal office draws up the

property settlement for both parties. We, as well as all lawyers we have dealt with, strongly encourage each party to retain his or her own attorney. The reasons are obvious.

2. Because the duties of military personnel may prevent them from defending themselves against a civil action (which includes divorce), the Soldiers' and Sailors' Civil Relief Act of 1940 (50 U.S.C. §§501-591) was enacted. This act protects active duty military from the entry of a default judgment or order against them. The Act requires that the plaintiff file an affidavit stating that the defendant is not in the armed services before a default order can be entered. If the plaintiff does not provide such a statement, then the court cannot enter a default judgment against the military member without appointing an attorney to represent the member. Failure to adhere to the requirements of the Soldiers' and Sailors' Civil Relief Act allows an active duty member to petition to set aside the judgment up to six months following discharge from the military. See Chapter 6 in the book, *Servicemember's Legal Guide, 2d edition* (listed in Appendix N of this book), for a more detailed explanation of this Act, along with a sample letter to request a delay in a lawsuit.

3. The most recently publicized case where the U.S. Supreme Court has applied the Soldiers' and Sailors' Civil Relief Act is that of Army Colonel Thomas Conroy. On March 31, 1993, the justices unanimously ruled that the Act provides blanket protection to servicemembers on active duty and that in the case of Colonel Conroy, the property of active duty members may not be seized for unpaid taxes, no matter why they did not pay. In an article in the April 19, 1993 issue of the *Air Force Times* (page 9), the opposing side was quoted: "The legitimate state, social and economic goals would be absolutely frustrated if a career serviceman is permitted to use (the act) to protect him from economic responsibilities he has voluntarily taken on." The Supreme Court did not agree with that reasoning, saying "it would not read an exception into the law where Congress has not put one." Editorial comment: In some respects, the *McCarty* decision elicited the same response from the Supreme

Court—it would not read a connotation of community property into the meaning of retired pay and if Congress wanted to change the intent, then it would have to pass new legislation.

10

SELECTING AN ATTORNEY

The Most Critical Step in Your Divorce

The most critical step you will take in your divorce, besides educating yourself on the USFSPA and the general legal requirements for divorce, will be your selection of an attorney. While retaining an attorney is not absolutely necessary in a divorce, it is the rare couple, indeed, who can agree to the division of all property and who know what tax or other legal implications may result from such a division. Notwithstanding the legal process involved in a divorce, there is the emotional trauma of one of the most stressful events in our lives (others being the death of a spouse or a child). Based on the personal stories we have heard, as well as reading on the subject, people in the process of divorce, men and women alike, are rarely able to tend to all the legal steps that must be followed. Maintaining your mental health becomes a number one priority. (See Appendix N for some suggested reading to help you cope with the emotional impact of divorce.)

You Are Still Responsible

Leaving the legal responsibilities to a competent attorney does not mean that you turn your life over to the attorney. The divorce is still your responsibility and it is you who must obtain and organize the information that the attorney will need.

We recommend that you find an attorney who specializes in domestic relations law, preferably divorce. It does not matter whether the attorney is male or female. What counts is what they know about military divorces, for it is rare, indeed, that the typical military person has any knowledge of the law in this area. (From the calls it gets, ARA is convinced that many lawyers are not knowledgeable on this subject, either.)

Don't Go to a Lawyer Who Does Not Specialize in Domestic Relations Law

You wouldn't go to a dentist to have your broken leg set in a cast, would you? The same advice follows for selecting a lawyer. There are many types of lawyers—some practice corporate law, others specialize in bankruptcy, and others specialize in dcmestic relations law, and even in the more specialized area of divorce.

Retain the services of an attorney who is absolutely knowledgeable and experienced in "military" divorces. Knowledge of domestic or family law is not enough; the attorney must be intimately familiar with military marriages, benefits, and military retirement and divorce law. Do not assume that just because the attorney is a former JAG (military lawyer, judge advocate general), that he or she knows about divorce law, let alone military divorce. They may not know the particular family law in the state where you will be obtaining a divorce, either.

Interviewing Attorneys

You will obviously have come up with some questions specific to your situation and should make a list of these before you interview your first attorney. Appendix L is a basic list of questions you will need to have answered on the first interview to determine whether you and your attorney will make a good "fit."

In general, your questions will deal with the following: the attorney's experience in handling military divorces, the attorney's general qualifications, the fee arrangements and administrative matters (how the attorney likes to work with the client).

Do not choose an attorney who is a family friend or who has had a close relationship with both you and your spouse. If upon mentioning phrases such as "SBP" and "combining your military retirement with a Civil Service retirement" you get a questioning look on the attorney's face, do not hesitate to terminate the interview. You are not there to train the lawyer.

One last point—if *you* feel uncomfortable with the attorney (i.e., you feel the attorney appears inexperienced, too young to comprehend the issues in a long-term marriage, not appreciative of a military career and retirement, or whatever the reason), and more particularly, if the attorney has not been able to answer your questions so you can understand them, *do not hire that attorney*. It is very important that you feel comfortable with the attorney. Firing an attorney is the choice of last resort, but you do need to realize when to cut your losses. Such situations only get worse if you decide later that you want to switch attorneys.

If you remember only one thing from this chapter, let it be that the attorney charges just as much for talking to you as for listening to you. Please keep in mind that you

are entering a business arrangement with the attorney—
the attorney is not your therapist or best friend. What you
perceive as a lack of empathy may be, for the most part,
an objective approach to your case for your sake. This is
not to say that the attorney should not acknowledge your
situation; but that your emotional investment is, by far,
your investment, and not your attorney's. The attorney's
job is to obtain the best and fairest settlement that will
allow both you and your spouse to continue on with your
lives in a manner as close as possible to what you en-
joyed during the marriage, and to do it in the shortest
possible time. Be advised that more and more attorneys
are charging their regular fee for initial consultation. We
feel that there should be no charge for a half-hour consultation (assuming you are organized, that may be all the
time you need). However, if you do have to pay, the money
will be well spent if all you learn is whether this attorney
is the right one for you. Sometimes you can determine
whether an attorney can handle your case by simply calling the attorney's office and asking.

Preparation—What You Need to Take to the Lawyer's Office

In Appendix M you will find a checklist for the things
you will need to provide an attorney. The checklist is also
excellent in helping you to prepare for an interview with
an attorney. Following is a summary of the information
you will need.

Basic Information

Be prepared to provide general information (for the
first interview) such as: how long you have been married, number of children and their ages, you and your

spouse's status relative to income, health, education, work experience, contribution to the marriage (monetary and nonmonetary). In short—the attorney needs to know what standard of living you have established and what is expected to happen to it once you are divorced. The attorney will also want to know the circumstances contributing to the divorce so that the grounds can be established.

Personal and Real Property

If you have never inventoried your assets (all of them—marital and nonmarital), you will need to in preparation for the divorce. You will also have to assess the fair market value of all your property. Some attorneys will advise you to assess what you think you could get for the property at a yard sale. If you have access to software such as "Managing Your Money" or "Quicken," you will find this task much easier.

Financial Status

The attorney will need to know your specific financial status, including what your monthly joint and separate budgets are. You can often obtain such forms from your local bank or credit union, or a realtor. Your attorney will also provide you the forms. You will have to provide, at least, a current copy of your Leave and Earnings Statement. If you are already retired, provide a copy of your monthly retiree's account statement. If you are a reservist, provide one of your weekend drill statements, as well as your most recent point accounting statement. Your income tax returns for the last 3 to 5 years will also be needed. Besides your monthly budget, you will have to list all your financial assets—savings accounts, bonds, IRAs, etc.

Summary of Military Service

The opposing attorney will no doubt require, under the process for obtaining information known as "discovery," a listing of your military assignments (when, where, how long), and whether your spouse accompanied you. So, now is a good time to compile such a list. Also indicate whether your spouse worked (and the approximate yearly income) for each assignment period. It is also important to know what the relative situation is for each spouse. Did your spouse take a traditional role in your family, while your career was the priority? If so, then your attorney will be better able to advise you of the local court's treatment of such marriages. Do you anticipate receiving disability and yet are still quite capable of working (and relatively young)? Will your spouse be eligible for military medical care, and commissary and exchange privileges? Such questions need to be addressed.

Preparation Is Necessary

All of this information will provide a better representation of the marital fiscal picture. The fact is that some attorneys are not experienced enough, or will not take on cases that have peculiar aspects. Thus, it is important that you not hold back information when discussing your case with an attorney. One attorney we know refuses to accept cases where the husband has committed adultery. Other attorneys do not handle divorces where child support is involved. Still others may need to refer you to another lawyer if domestic violence is involved.

Each case is different, and the lawyer you interview should be able to tell you, from your information and questions, whether he or she can handle your case with the least amount of complications.

11

YOUR
STRATEGIES

Many military members have asked for a step-by-step guide to the USFSPA and their divorce. Every situation is different and no one publication will be able to answer all your questions or even apply in every instance to your particular case. No book or attorney can make your decisions for you—you will have to do that. As you consider the ramifications of a divorce in light of your military service, there are some strategies you can essay. As you review them, keep in mind that ARA does not endorse a win-lose situation (unless it is couched in the facetious terms that the only winners in a divorce are the lawyers), although we realize that many divorces end up in such a battle. The ARA's position is that these matters should be based on merit, need, and the ability to pay.

Further, the ARA believes in the fair and equitable treatment of *both* members of a military marriage that ends in divorce.

Legal and Moral Obligations in a Divorce

As we have pointed out several times, the military member and spouse have both moral and legal obligations when it comes to the family. The most important *legal* matters that a divorce will resolve will be the division of your property; decisions on where your children will live, who will care for them, and how they will be cared for; and the distribution of income between the spouses. While it would be nice for you to discuss all the terms of your divorce settlement with your spouse in an amicable manner, we realize that is not always possible.

Considerations and Approaches

Just as discussions regarding the divorce settlement with your spouse may not always be pleasant, neither will the negotiation sessions go so well when either side is ill informed about the law as it relates to divorce involving a military member. If the decision to divorce has been made, then there are some steps you can take to make it as simple as possible.

Suggested Strategies

1. GET AN EDUCATED LAWYER.

This is advised earlier in this book; but it is repeated because it is important. It is imperative that you retain the services of an attorney who is absolutely knowledgeable on this subject. Knowledge of domestic or family law is not enough; the attorney must be intimately familiar with military marriages, benefits, and military retirement and divorce law.

Finding an attorney who is knowledgeable on military divorces may not be easy. If you cannot find such a person, you will have to educate your attorney on the USFSPA before you go to court. *That* can be an expensive endeavor.

Also, while you may get references from other people, keep in mind that the facts of your case may not be the same as those of your friend or reference. You may have details that complicate your case beyond the experience of that attorney. Moreover, there is a thing called "lawyer-client chemistry."

Some people advocate finding the best lawyer possible, despite the fact that such a person may also be the most expensive. A very experienced lawyer could save you money by not having to research everything to "get educated." A good lawyer can cut the time it takes to bring your divorce to closure because he or she has a reputation for "cutting to the chase," or perhaps intimidating other lawyers.

You may want to sit in on some cases in the courtroom, or find out whether there are any retired men or women in your area who conduct courtroom observations. We know of one woman in Fairfax County, Virginia, who regularly attends domestic relations court. She can tell you how each divorce attorney performs and how the judges act.

The final choice of an attorney is yours. If you are comfortable with the lawyer you have interviewed and selected (i.e., the attorney's knowledge of military divorce, a grasp of your situation particulars, and sufficient experience to proceed in an expeditious manner), then it probably may not matter that the attorney you have chosen is not the "best" in the region.

2. THE USFSPA IS A "PERMISSIVE LAW."

While some state courts have automatically been awarding 50 percent of the military member's retired pay to the former spouse, you shouldn't throw in the towel prematurely. The USFSPA states that they *may* treat the retired pay as property and award a portion to the former spouse, up to 50 percent (65 percent with child support).

Unlike civilian divorces where property division is often based on a number of factors, including financial and economic need, the USFSPA does not require the military spouse to prove either in order to receive a portion of the military retirement pay. Do not throw it in the hopper voluntarily with no attempt to negotiate a more reasonable (for you) settlement.

3. COURT RULINGS ON RETIRED PAY WHILE ON ACTIVE DUTY.

Federal law (the USFSPA) provides that you cannot be ordered to retire involuntarily so that payments to a former spouse can begin. Nor does the USFSPA allow a court to order the military member to begin payments (i.e., distributions from active duty pay) while you are still on active duty.[1] Nor are USFSPA payments authorized after recall of retired military members to active duty. You cannot collect retired pay, or pay it out, unless you are retired. You can, of course, be ordered to pay alimony or child support, with the source not specified.

4. DO NOT FORGET THE DENOMINATOR.

The computation that many states are now using to determine what pro rata share will go to the spouse is based on the number of years the spouse was married to you while you were in the military (creditable time, the numerator), divided by your total current military time *at the time of the divorce* (the denominator). The longer you stay in the military before retiring, the more favorable the formula (fraction) under which your retirement pay will be divided.

An illustration of this type of calculation would work like this (and is the case in many courts):

> *At the time of divorce, a couple was married for 12 years concurrently with military service; the military member had served 20 years at time of retirement. The calculation would be:*

$$12/20 \ x \ .50 = 30\% \ to \ spouse$$

> *If, on the other hand, the military member stays in for 30 years, the calculation would be 12/30 x .50 = 20% to spouse.*
>
> *This might, of course, be offset by promotions after divorce if the final divorce decree did not specify that the ex-spouse's share was to be calculated at the pay grade extant at the time of divorce.*

5. KNOW THE LAW REGARDING DISABILITY PAY—USFSPA DOES NOT AWARD IT.

As affirmed by the U.S. Supreme Court decision in *Mansell v. Mansell* (1989), the USFSPA does not authorize a court to include disability pay in the definition of "disposable pay" if the disability pay is being received under Chapter 61 of 10 U.S.C. §1201 et seq. However, some states have ignored the law in this area.

If the court does award your disability pay, you probably have an appealable case. Consult an attorney.

6. CONSIDER INCOME TAX IMPLICATIONS.

Your bottom line (as well as your spouse's) is affected by the effective date of your divorce, not your retirement date. If your divorce occurred before February 5, 1991, then your check was based on all the tax liability (both of you) being taken from your check prior to dividing it with the spouse. The spouse still has to pay tax on his or her share.[2] If your divorce occurred on or after February 5, 1991 (Public Law 101-510, §555), then each of you will be responsible for your own taxes.

The amount of your retirement pay paid to your ex-spouse is tax deductible for you. Conversely, your ex-spouse must pay income tax on what he or she receives.

7.   IF YOU WERE DIVORCED ON OR PRIOR TO JUNE 25, 1981.

If you were divorced on or prior to June 25, 1981 *and* your final decree did not make an award of your retirement pay *or* reserve the option of the court to later make an award, your ex-spouse cannot exploit the USFSPA to force you into ex-post facto payments.

Unfortunately, some courts are ignoring Public Law 101-510 §555, which provides this protection. If the court ignores this amendment to the USFSPA, you may have an appealable case.[3] The point of law is federal supremacy. Under the supremacy clause of the U.S. Constitution, federal law prevails over state law when the two are in direct conflict.

You and your attorney may wish to remove the case to a federal court, since an appeal to a higher state court may well result in an affirmation of a lower court's erroneous ruling. Your counsel should check your state courts' record in this regard vis-a-vis USFSPA matters.

8.   AVOID WINDFALL BENEFITS.

If you are divorcing while on active duty, make sure

your decree states that payments after you retire will be based on your pay grade at the time of divorce. You will probably have to include COLAs (understandably), but that is probably better than payments based on the pay grade at which you finally retire.

If you are already retired and the spouse whom you divorced at a lower pay grade takes you into court asking for USFSPA payments, insist that they be calculated at the pay grade in effect at the time of divorce.

9. CONSIDER A SEPARATION AGREEMENT.

If you have the time and the relationship permits, it may be possible to execute a separation agreement which addresses all the issues (e.g., division of property, alimony, child support, etc.) before going into court. This permits a rational approach to problems in the presence of counsel (separate counsel for each recommended) in a more relaxed environment than a courtroom.

Moreover, it can result in settlements based on full discussion and negotiation, rather than the (snap) decisions of a judge who may be given an incomplete picture of the circumstances and issues of the divorce. Most courts will accept a properly executed separation agreement as the basis for a final divorce settlement. A separation agreement can reduce costs, save time, and minimize the possibility of misunderstandings later on.

10. DON'T FORGET SBP, LIFE INSURANCE, AND OTHER SURVIVOR BENEFITS.

Your spouse may be entitled to coverage under the Survivor Benefit Plan. If she or he is awarded SBP, you are allowed to deduct the amount of the SBP premiums from your USFSPA payments (and they come "off the top," before your tax liability is computed). You will not be able to deduct (for income tax purposes) the premiums on any commercial life insurance for which your ex-spouse is the beneficiary *unless* she or he is the legal owner of the policies. Survivor benefits are very important to ex-spouses and may be important negotiating chips for you in any pre-divorce negotiations.

11.   KEEP YOURSELF INFORMED.

Your divorce strategy is inextricably tied to the law as it exists at the time of your divorce. Changes to the USFSPA are under constant consideration. Many attorneys for the spouses are including in the divorce decree language that allows the spouse to return to court to receive additional benefits, should the law change.[4]

While such changes might not necessarily change the net due to you,[5] you could find yourself facing additional expenses as the attorneys work out the appropriate wording, or the spouse causes additional work that incurs legal fees. To protect yourself, you may want to include language that states that whatever additional changes are incurred, the party filing same also pays the legal fees and related costs.

One of the ways you can keep yourself informed is by becoming a member of the ARA. Its weekly telephone update service can keep you informed of upcoming legislative events that could work to both your and your spouse's advantage in a divorce. Its bimonthly newsletter is another excellent source.

Another way is to spend an afternoon in your local law library, reading the section on divorce code, and reviewing representative cases. If you need help on where to go or what to search, the ARA can provide some guidance.

You can also consult with local groups about divorce procedures in your area. Men's as well as women's groups, including women's centers (often open to men) and county agencies provide free information (and often seminars) on divorce procedural requirements. A call to your county court offices can also yield a lot of information.

12. GET ORGANIZED AND KNOW WHEN TO CUT YOUR LOSSES.

While we would like to think this is not true, no one has stepped forward to refute the following rule:

> *"Whatever it is, it will always take longer than you had expected, cost more than you had expected, and produce results you had not expected."* *And its close relative: "When you need it, you won't be able to find it."*

One of the interpretations of this is that "time is money"—most often, yours. A divorce creates an extremely stressful situation. Matters are further compounded by all the factors affecting military couples that are discussed in this book. Approaching your divorce with due regard to the emotional and mental health aspects of the situation in an organized manner will help you immensely. Many people have told us that it was not until some time after their divorce that they realized that during the process they had performed quite irrationally. Be aware that this can happen and keep a constant check on your emotions and thought processes. Appendix N lists some books that may be of help in this regard.

The following are some basic steps you should take to get organized and stay organized. Doing so can save you money and aggravation.

A. Keep a log book.

Organize it by date—enter all major actions in your case *as they happen*. Include the times (beginning and ending) and dates you talk with your attorney, when your attorney says he or she has talked or written something to your spouse's attorney, and when your attorney has gone to court on your behalf. Sometimes the only way you will become aware of such information is through telephone conversations or other oral communications. Log it while it is still clear in your mind.

B. Establish a file box.

Get an empty box or plastic file container (preferably one with handles) and a bunch of file folders. The following are the *minimum* number of categories you should have. Label them as follows:

SUSPENSE FILE
Keep a record of any tasks assigned to you by your attorney and a record of what you do about them. Also note any special dates (hearings, meetings with your spouse's attorney). If your attorney (or opposing attorney) has said he or she will do something (you might find this in a piece of correspondence), note it in this file. Deadlines are critical in legal actions. Missing deadlines can be catastrophic.

CORRESPONDENCE TO/FROM ATTORNEY
This file also includes copies of correspondence the opposing attorney sends to your attorney. Note the receipt dates in your log book.

COURT DOCUMENTS
This file holds the papers that your attorney and opposing attorney have filed with the court, e.g., petition, motions, temporary orders.

NOTES/LETTERS FROM YOUR SPOUSE
If you and your spouse are on speaking terms (even if hostile), include in this folder any letters, notes of phone conversations, etc. Do this even if you are under restraining orders not to communicate or if your attorney has instructed you not to communicate. Those restraints may not apply to your spouse and what you receive may be useful.

FINANCIAL DATA (see Appendix M)
This folder might be subdivided into several folders that contain the following: income statement (monthly budget—what you receive and spend, your living expenses), copies of income tax records for last three years, complete financial disclosure, etc.

BILLINGS (FROM ATTORNEY)
(other labels: Invoices, Statements)
Put the statements you receive from your attorney into this file. Also include the retainer letter or statement you initially executed regarding the fee arrangement. If you don't have one, be sure to confirm in writing with your attorney the arrangements you have agreed to (and put that letter in this file). If there is any misunderstanding later on, you want to be sure to get it cleared up as quickly as possible. When you receive a statement, cross check it with your

log and the correspondence (including court papers) you have received in the last 30 days.

Lawyers can and do make billing mistakes—careful checking can result in significant savings. Do not hesitate to query your attorney about billing inconsistencies. Generally, they are more than willing to correct a mistake in your favor. Put your inquiry in writing and include a copy of the bill. Your attorney should be billing you monthly in detail, by listing the date, description of activity, and time involved. If you are not receiving monthly bills, then be sure to bring this to your attorney's attention. DO NOT LET GRASS GROW when it comes to legal bills.

For more complicated divorce cases, you should consider designing (or having someone design) an automated database to track information, particularly if you or your attorney expects protracted litigation.[6]

A file plan such as this will keep you organized and on track with your divorce actions. Such a structure and methodology will also signal when there is something awry with the legal representation you are receiving and the course your divorce is taking. By educating yourself and listening to your instincts, you will usually know when you need to pull in the reins and, if necessary, switch attorneys.

Military members, in our experience, frequently forget that the attorney is working for them and that attorneys can be dismissed and replaced when the representation is not getting the job done or the lawyer-client chemistry is not right . . . BUT, make sure your problem is with the attorney and not your misperceptions of what he or she should be able to do for you.[7]

Never forget that *you* are responsible for your divorce. Your attorney's duty is to counsel and advise you and then represent you in decisions which remain *your* responsibility to make.

If you are unsure of what is happening (and the fact that things not going your way is not necessarily a reason for firing your attorney), the ARA can help you.

One Final Note About Records

Our advice on how long the file on your divorce should be kept is **FOREVER**. Some attorneys do shift law firms and areas of the law in which they work. Many people have told us that the principal reason they prevailed when their divorce case was reopened unexpectedly was that *their* files contained the information they needed.

Remember—there is *no* statute of limitations on the time allowed for your ex-spouse to petition for your retirement pay if he or she was not awarded it at the time of divorce. Your file may contain something urgently needed for that reopening.

Summary

There are really only three things you have to do: find yourself a knowledgeable lawyer, know the essence of the law yourself, and get organized. Doing these three things will solve the one problem we have found that is pervasive with military divorces, whether it is the military member or the spouse: they found out they had an incompetent lawyer and they did not know about the law until *after* the fact, i.e., when an appeal was taken or the divorce was reopened for clarification, modification, or enforcement.

CHAPTER ENDNOTES

1. This provision of the federal law could be interpreted differently in New Mexico courts. (This statement is made because New

Mexico has ignored federal law with respect to military retired pay in divorce cases.) The state now favors "finality" in divorce cases, as ruled in *Ruggles v. Ruggles*, __NM__, 860 P.2d 182 (1993), that where there is a "vested" retirement fund, the attitude is to have the money divided. (Some states have defined the term "vested" to include a retirement where there is no actual monetary investment, such as in the military retired pay system.) This "finality" appears to contradict New Mexico's own reasoning cited in numerous other cases in that, under New Mexico law, there is a "limited reservation of jurisdiction" that is incorporated into every divorce. In other words, the courts are saying it is "OK" to reopen a case at any time for any reason, and that changes in federal law do not preempt or have any authority over New Mexico law. What this could mean to military members is that, at least in New Mexico, the court could order the military member to begin payments of not-yet received retired pay. See Chapter 2, endnote #1.

2. While this is double taxation to the spouse (for pre-February 1991 divorces), it is considered legal by the IRS. (See *Eatinger v. Commissioner of Internal Revenue*, US TC, TC Memo 1990-310, June 20, 1990, 16 FLR 1399.) The IRS does, in reality, collect taxes *twice* on the spouse's share. We do not have any data for cases where the divorce took place *before* February 1991, but the property settlement was not executed until *after* February 1991. We know of one case, however, where the court has been asked to adjudicate the property using the post-February 1991 definition of retired pay (November 1990 amendment to the USFSPA). The particulars of this case, however, are such that the divorce was granted in one state in 1986, with the property settlement begun in another state five years later, and property scattered in three states. The parties reside in different states. Given the legwork that would have to be done to calculate the various years' worth of retired pay for tax purposes, it is no wonder that attorneys for both parties are in agreement that using the February 1991 definition of retired pay is only common sense. It goes without saying that "time is of the essence."

3. As mentioned in endnote #1, New Mexico has ignored the retroactivity amendment as ruled in *Berry v. Meadows*, NMCA No. 14,907, October 14, 1993 (Memorandum Opinion), cert.

den. November 24, 1993 (the Court of Appeals affirmed the trial court's ruling—unpublished opinion); and in *Gonzales v. Roybal*, Civ. No. 93-1302MV, U.S.D.C.N.M. (currently on appeal).

4. We do not mean here the future changes to your income that allow a spouse to reopen a divorce case because "circumstances have changed," as many state courts allow. The changes referred to here are strictly those related to military retired pay and benefits.

5. For example, if the law changed to allow more former spouses to use various military benefits, e.g., the commissary, such a change would not affect the amount of money either of you currently receives from your retirement check.

6. ARA can put you in touch with experienced personnel to design an automated database for you. The time involved averages 1-3 hours.

7. Consult the excellent book, *Using a Lawyer . . . And What To Do If Things Go Wrong* (see Appendix N).

12

LEGISLATIVE ENVIRONMENT: MARITAL MINEFIELD OR SMOOTH SAILING?

From 1982 forward, there was virtually no change to the Uniformed Services Former Spouses' Protection Act, with the exception of some benefits that did not affect the military retiree's pay.[1] Then, the activity picked up again in 1989.

For the Military Retiree

In the first session of the 101st Congress (1990), three bills in favor of the military retiree were introduced by Representative Robert Dornan (R-CA), H.R. 572, 2277, 2300:

H.R. 572	Terminate the spouse's property interest in military retirement benefits in the event of remarriage subsequent to divorce from the member.

H.R. 2277   Bar states from awarding a portion of military retirement benefits paid to a former spouse upon a member's eligibility for retirement.

H.R. 2300   Change the definition of "disposable retired or retainer pay."

For the Spouse

A fourth bill, H.R. 3776 (introduced by Rep. Patricia Schroeder, D-CO) would have further strengthened a former spouse's claims for a pro rata share of the retired pay, including VA disability compensation. This bill contained several components, including the establishment of a rebuttable presumption that a divorcing spouse would receive a pro rata division of military retired pay if there were no court order or spousal agreement and the couple was married at least 10 years.

It would also have allowed the former spouse to continue receiving a share of retired pay even if the member returned to active duty or forfeited part of a retired pay check in order to provide survivor benefits coverage. Former spouses claimed that the current law allowed a retiree to shield some retirement income from division with a former spouse.

H.R. 3776   Contained several components: establishment of rebuttable presumption that a divorcing spouse will receive a pro rata share of military retirement benefits, mandate division of military retirement benefits, prevention of duplicate benefits, elimination of the "disposable" limitation to make the division of "gross" military retired pay, and elimination of the 10-year marriage limitation for direct payment.

April 1990 House Hearings and Results in the 1991 Defense Authorization Bill

Hearings were held before the House Armed Services Subcommittee on Military Personnel and Compensation, on April 4, 1990. Testimony in favor of the spouse was presented by the National Organization for Women (NOW), Ex-Partners of Servicemen (women) for Equality (EX-POSE), the American Bar Association, and the National Military Family Association. Testimony in favor of the military retiree was presented by the American Retirees Association, The American Legion, the Military Coalition (by The Retired Officers Association), and the Non-Commissioned Officers Association.

ARA produced "An Assessment of the Impact of the USFSPA," April 1990. The (then) Deputy Assistant Secretary of Defense for Military Manpower and Personnel Policy testified for the Department of Defense.

Only one provision favorable to the military member was addressed by Congress, that of prohibiting the reopening of divorce cases completed before June 25, 1981 (and which did not treat or reserve jurisdiction to treat any amount of retired pay as property of the member and spouse).

In favor of the spouse, the House Armed Services Committee changed the definition of disposable retired pay to exclude taxes and other levies from the definition. (In some cases, this change was a positive move for the member, as it eliminated paperwork and confusion relative to the payment of taxes between the two parties.)

Retroactivity Finally Laid to Rest

The FY 1991 Defense Authorization Act clarified several matters, with the advantage to the former spouse in some cases, and to the military member in others.

In the fall of 1990, some progress toward equity was finally realized by the military retiree, ending the discriminatory retroactive USFSPA provisions. The amendment,[2] passed on November 5, 1990, benefited the military member by doing away with the ability to reopen a divorce case just to decide the military retirement pay issue and, thereby, causing unexpected tremendous financial loss.

H.R. 4739 §555, Public Law 101-510 (National Defense Authorization Act). Finally ended the discriminatory retroactive military USFSPA provisions, but not until November 5, 1992.[3]

Disposable Pay Redefined for Divorces Final After February 4, 1991

Public Law 101-510 embodied another amendment to the USFSPA which affected military members and their ex-spouses. For divorces that became final after February 4, 1991, the definition of disposable retired pay was significantly changed. Basically, few debts and no income taxes can be withheld before the former spouse's share is calculated. This change does not affect retirees whose divorces were final before the effective date or for those making USFSPA payments out of pocket.[4]

Perhaps one of the key reasons for such a change has been the tax court case, *Eatinger v. Commissioner of Internal Revenue,* U.S. Tax Court Dkt. No. 16564-89 (1990). Regardless of when the divorce took place, military retirement benefits are included as gross income to the recipient spouse as well as to the military member. The retirement income was characterized as deferred compensation to the military member and not a transfer of community property to the spouse. Thus, the spouse who was divorced prior to February 5, 1991 was penalized twice for taxes.

In cases where the ex-spouse is being paid directly by a military finance center, this change does simplify the whole issue of tax liability (and subsequent paperwork) for both parties, with neither party having to communicate with the other at tax time. Both parties now receive statements of income from the Defense Accounting and Finance Service, showing what income from the military retired pay was received and the taxes that were withheld. The reporting form, called IRS Form 1099-R, replaces IRS Form W-2P.[5] While this may create the impression that income taxes are being paid on *income*, they are, in fact, being paid on *property*.

Protection for Abused Military Dependents and Former Spouses

Legislation was passed in the National Defense Authorization Act for FY 1993, Public Law 102-484,[6] that provides annuities for former spouses of military members who become disqualified for retired pay due to abuse of a dependent. Known as the Abused Military Dependents Act (AMDA) of 1992, the statute requires the military services to pay an annuity, based on the retirement pay to which the military member would otherwise have qualified, to eligible spouses and former spouses.[7] Qualified dependents are also eligible for dental and medical care, and commissary, exchange, and other military base privileges.[8].

Although the purpose of this bill is laudatory, it must be noted that it is attached as subsection (h) to 10 U.S.C. §1408, "Benefits for dependents who are victims of abuse by members losing right to retired pay." This means that within the same section of Title 10 of the U.S. Code, there are conflicting provisions for the treatment of ex-spouses of military members. The most notable of these apply to remarriage and to the abused ex-spouse's entitlement to benefits beyond retirement pay.

The table on page 113 is a brief summary of the differences between this add-on provision and the remainder of the USFSPA.

Fairness Amendments

On May 2, 1991, Representative Robert K. Dornan (R-CA) introduced H.R. 2200, the "Uniformed Services Former Spouses' Protection Act Fairness Amendments of 1991." This legislation[9] resulted from the hearings held in 1990 by the House Armed Services Subcommittee on Personnel and Compensation. Its objectives were to:

1. Terminate payments of retired pay upon the remarriage of former military spouses;
2. Restrict awards under USFSPA to an amount or percentage of the military member's pay at the time of the divorce (not at the time of retirement);
3. Establish a 2-year statute of limitations for former spouses to seek a division of retired pay from the time of divorce; and ensure that jurisdiction of a court to hear a subsequent action to divide the retired pay is established independently of the jurisdiction of the court at the time of the original divorce action;[10]
4. Reaffirm the current prohibition on division of veterans' disability pay; and

5. Prohibit the courts from ordering any payments under USFSPA from active duty pay.

Although the support individual military members
gave to Rep. Dornan was commendable, this legislation
lacked the cosponsors needed for the bill to be enacted.
Further, the House Armed Services Committee did not
receive very much mail on the subject, thereby giving the
impression that enacting this reform legislation was not
a high priority.[11]

What Is on the Legislative Horizon

Just as passage of the Fairness Amendments is a priority agenda for the ARA in the 1990s, it is expected that
opponents will not only introduce legislation[12] to block
these equitable changes but also introduce other legislation as well. Such pro ex-spouse proposals would most
likely include:

• Make the Public Law 101-510 definition of disposable pay (i.e., pre-tax) retroactive to cover those
  ex-spouses divorced prior to February 5, 1991. To
  this end, Rep. Schroeder introduced H.R. 2258 and
  H.R. 2790 in the 103rd Congress.

• Provide a spouse with automatic, statutory entitlement to the member's military retirement pay. (This
  would be irrespective of any considerations in re-
  lation to divorce.)

• Provide shopping privileges for 20-20-15s. (It is not
  known what comparable provisions ex-spouses
  would endorse for those military members separated
  prior to 20 years of service.)

- Provide ex-spouse statutory entitlement to separation bonus payout monies (i.e., SSB and VSI) as property. To do this, Rep. Schroeder introduced H.R. 3574 in the 103rd Congress.

- Allow a former spouse who was an original SBP beneficiary (prior to divorce) to receive the benefits if the military retiree dies without a current beneficiary or if the second marriage ends in divorce.

Abused Dependents Add-On	Remainder of USFSPA
Original bill provided 1-year statute of limitations on application for payments. Eliminated in conference.	No statute of limitations on application by former spouse.
Fault is a determinant.	Fault is not considered. Rewards miscreant spouses of military members.
Fairness is an issue.	Fairness not considered.
Terminates payments upon remarriage of ex-spouse. Payments resume if remarriage terminated by death or divorce. (Original version also terminated payments upon cohabitation.)	**Payments continue until death of military member or benefitting ex-spouse, even if the ex-spouse remarries.**
Possible incentive for fraudulent claims.	No incentive for fraud because USFSPA award is a no-fault process.
Expenses borne by the government.	No expense to government beyond amounts regularly appropriated for military retirement pay. Payment comes out of the amount the military member receives.
While possible, "windfall benefits" not likely.	"Windfall benefits" regularly provided to ex-spouses, particularly in ex post facto USFSPA awards.

Summary of differences between the AMDA add-on provisions and the remainder of the USFSPA.

CHAPTER ENDNOTES

1.   There have been many changes to SBP—just about every year—which may or may not figure in the military member's divorce settlement. The best coverage on SBP can be found in The Retired Officers Association booklet on SBP. See Appendix N.

2.   The change came in markup to the National Defense Authorization Act.

3.   The original entry was for the amendment to become effective 90 days after being signed into law. Unbeknown to its sponsor, Rep. Dornan, it was learned that another change had been slipped into the final version, delaying the effective date by two years.

4.   On May 25, 1993, Rep. Schroeder introduced legislation (H.R. 2258) to make this provision apply retroactively to *all* military divorces. In other words, her bill would allow former spouses already awarded a portion of retired pay as part of the property settlement to go back to court to get the payments recomputed. Such payments would, however, be prospective and not retroactive. In the spring of 1993, this bill was withdrawn during subcommittee markup deliberations, but may later be reintroduced in subcommittee by another member of Congress with additional language adding SSB and VSI payments as marital property. Such a provision would create mass confusion for already retired members, while providing additional monies to lawyers who would see this as a "windfall" opportunity. *Rep. Schroeder is proposing here to ignore what two people have already agreed upon in a court of law.*

It would be totally unfair to the military member to change the wording in a decree that may have been issued years ago. People plan their lives based on the amount of income they are receiving, and *such an enormous change could wreak havoc in a long-lasting domino effect:* loan applications in progress, mortgage payments, child support and alimony payments to former spouses, share of college tuition expenses for children, and more. Whatever income the member might be receiving as a result of the definition for retired pay at the time of the divorce is, to be sure, taxed to the member. Where states allow spouses to reserve or apply for additional support based on changed circumstances, then such remedies are already available to the former spouse. We see here, once again, a situation where the federal government ought not to meddle in the domestic relations laws of the individual states.

5. The retiree's form 1099-R (the name of this form is *Distributions from Pensions, Annuities, Retirement or Profit Sharing Plans, IRAs, Insurance Contracts, Etc.*) shows taxes withheld for the amount of retired pay the retiree receives. The ex-spouse's form shows taxes withheld from any retired pay a military finance center pays to the ex-spouse as property divided under a court order. The amounts a retiree pays to a former spouse as alimony, child support, or as a voluntary allotment continue to be reported as income received by the retiree and appear on the retiree's 1099-R form.

6. This was a stand-alone bill, S. 3009, introduced by Senator Pete Domenici (R-NM).

7. Payments come out of funds in the Department of Defense Military Retirement Fund, as established by section 1461 of Title 10, U.S.C.

8. The Defense Department's family advocacy program stated there were 23,343 reports of child abuse in 1992, of which 44 percent were substantiated. There were also 23,872 cases of spouse abuse in 1992, of which 76 percent were substantiated. Additional bills targeting domestic violence in the military were introduced (summer 1993) by Rep. Jon Kyl (R-AZ), and some were included in the National Defense Authorization Act for FY 1994.

9. This bill has been revised and is now titled, "Divorced Military Members' Equity Amendments of 1993."

10. An example of this is: Parties assigned under orders to Alaska, consent to the jurisdiction of Alaska courts to secure a divorce

decree. The court fails to divide retired pay. The servicemember subsequently retires and moves to a permanent residence in Florida while the ex-spouse moves to a permanent residence in Massachusetts. Subsequent action by the ex-spouse to divided retired pay should be brought in Florida, not Alaska.

11. Many people do not think that their "one little letter" can make a difference, but it can. Constituency mail, obviously, does have an impact. A sincere, handwritten letter is generally thought to be the most effective.

12. Rep. Patricia Schroeder introduced H.R. 3574 in the first session of the 103rd Congress. The bill would amend Title 10, U.S.C., to provide improved benefits for former spouses of servicemembers who are voluntarily or involuntarily discharged during the downsizing of the Defense Department. She is proposing that the separation pay be subject to division as marital property in a divorce.

13

ABOUT THE ARA

What and Where

The American Retirees Association (ARA) was formed in 1984 to defend the rights of active duty, reserve, and retired servicemembers in divorce. ARA publishes a bi-monthly newsletter for members to keep them informed of pending legislation and other actions affecting the service member's retired pay relative to divorce.

ARA also sends out special notices when it needs to alert the membership about an important congressional action or to write to Congress.

Chartered in California as a tax-exempt corporation #1551226, ARA has also been granted federal tax exemption status I.D. 33-0246746. Dues are $25 a year and they are tax deductible, as are any contributions to the ARA. The Washington operations office is staffed weekdays from 8:00 a.m. to 4:00 p.m., ET. Both ARA offices are staffed by volunteers.

The addresses are:

Headquarters ARA	Washington Operations ARA
7564 Trade Street	2009 N. 14th St. Suite 300
San Diego, CA 92121-2412	Arlington, VA 22201-2514
Tel: (619) 239-9000	Tel: (703) 527-3065

If You Have Any Questions

Inquiries relating to dues, membership, publications, etc., should be directed to the headquarters office in San Diego. All other matters should be directed to the Washington operations office.

ARA operates a weekly telephone update service. By calling 1-900-420-3714, program 111, you can hear about upcoming legislative events and keep current on the laws and other actions affecting military retirees relative to a divorce. There is a charge for this call ($2.00 per minute, of which $1.00 goes to the ARA treasury). The average message is three minutes, with a maximum of five minutes. A Touch-Tone® telephone is required.

The ARA's Platform

The ARA's pursuit of USFSPA reform is based on a platform of fairness and equity for *both* members of a military marriage that ends in divorce. The ARA believes that divorce settlements should be based on merit, need, and ability to pay—not blind adherence to an unfair, discriminatory law which implies that the military spouse is invariably blameless while the military member always "wears the black hat" in a divorce proceeding. This may change when affected (and possibly traumatized) female military members appear in divorce court to defend against making USFSPA payments to their civilian, male ex-spouses, but it has not happened yet.

ARA's Proposals for Reform of the USFSPA

The following proposals for reform are based on input from the military and civilian community.

1. Terminate USFSPA payments upon the remarriage of the benefitting ex-spouse. Terminate current payments to remarried former spouses not more than 180 days from the date of enactment of the amendment.

2. Restrict awards under the USFSPA to correspond to the military member's length of service and pay grade at the time of divorce, not at the time of retirement. USFSPA payments would, however, be adjusted to existing pay scales at the time of retirement.

3. Establish a statute of limitations giving former spouses two years from the date of a final divorce to seek a division of military retirement pay under the USFSPA.

4. Reinforce that provision of the USFSPA which precludes the inclusion of disability pay in the calculation of disposable pay. Consider, however, the inclusion of disability pay where military retired pay is the *only* asset of the marriage.

5. Provide specific wording to protect active duty military personnel by precluding:

- Involuntary court-ordered retirements in order to commence USFSPA payments.
- Distribution of active duty pay pursuant to court orders under the USFSPA.
- USFSPA payments after recall of retired military members to active duty.

6. Preclude retroactive application of the USFSPA for any divorce finalized prior to February 1, 1983, the effective date of the USFSPA. Public Law 101-510 of

(November 5, 1990) prohibits retroactive opening of divorces final on and before June 25, 1981, one day before the U.S. Supreme Court *McCarty* decision. This denies relief for those divorced during the "gap" period between *McCarty* and the effective date of the USFSPA. The failure to grandfather the USFSPA was a manifest injustice to military people who had served honorably prior to February 1, 1983 and who were preemptively deprived of their matured right to *full* retirement pay.

7. Require the leadership of the uniformed services to brief their personnel on the existence and significance of the USFSPA.

Afterthought

It is very important to constantly revisit the USFSPA and to reexamine the premises underlying its enactment. This should occur in the light of evolving social, economic, and cultural changes which have substantially altered the status of the military spouse of the early 1980s.

The history of the USFSPA provides irrefutable evidence that it unfairly discriminates against divorcing military marital partners who, manifestly, do *not* enjoy protection under the law equal to that provided their civilian counterparts. An interesting aspect of the USFSPA's treatment of military women is that virtually all the resistance to its reform emanates from the feminist sector.

An overwhelming majority of the national community of veterans' organizations, with an aggregate membership over 10,000,000, support reform of the USFSPA to resolve its inequities. Some (e.g., The American Legion) even advocate its repeal.

Somehow, members of the uniformed services of both sexes must convince their 1990s contemporaries that they are not looking for a *win* in a divorce court, just a *tie*.

14

RESTORING FAIRNESS AND EQUALITY TO THE MILITARY DIVORCE PROCESS

Why No Further Equity Changes to the USFSPA?

Perhaps you may be wondering why further equity changes have not been made to this law. You might want to ask yourself what part you may have had, not only in how the law came about but why no further changes (except for the November 5, 1990 retroactivity halt) have been made to bring about equity.

Congress Does Not Operate in a Vacuum

We find some lessons learned in the legislative process here. First, laws are not made without going through a very structured process. When the law is one that affects a lot of people, such as the COLA for military retirees, you can be sure that various military and veterans' organizations will not only be tracking such legislation, but will also be publicizing it to their membership. Indeed, rules and procedures[1] that further clarify whatever legislation is passed are first published (as well as proposed changes) in the *Federal Register*, during which time the general public has the opportunity to comment.

Thus, with regard to USFSPA, there was congressional testimony published[2] that anyone could have read, but evidently few did—or, if they did, decided the law was too unreasonable to have much chance of enactment.

Keeping Up to Date on Important Issues

Second, many of our elected officials publish a constituent-oriented newsletter or update bulletin which highlights new and proposed changes to laws. The question you should be asking yourself then (be it the issue of divorce law or environmental problems) is: When was the last time you let your representative know how you stood on a particular issue? Further, do you know how that person feels about a particular issue or law? Is that individual even remotely aware a problem exists?

On March 10, 1993, the House Budget Committee first passed legislation calling for COLA caps for military retirees. Until April 1, 1993, when debates in Congress ended, your Pentagon leadership remained silent. Why? Lobbyists for organizations representing the service members and retirees said the reason was "the lack of support from uniformed and civilian Pentagon leaders."[3]

Civics 101 — Congress Does Not Have to Be Consistently Fair

In the same *Air Force Times* article on the COLA caps, one can find another similarity to USFSPA. Some groups have been spared from COLA limits, just as some federal retirees (notably some employees of the Foreign Service and the Central Intelligence Agency) were exempt from having the payments to the former spouse deducted from their retired pay. This was another case of a similar program (i.e., federal retirement) that was not extended to military retirees. Quoting retired Air Force Colonel Paul W. Arcari, [then] director of legislative affairs for The Retired Officers Association, "The fact that federal police and air traffic controllers were protected but military members were not [the former were spared the COLA caps] is a sign that we did not get our message across."[4]

Read It in Your Military Newspaper First!

In some respects, then, the same thing (call it apathy in some cases) could be said regarding USFSPA recognition, although with some differences. First of all, while the coverage has been limited, the various service *Times* (Air Force, Army, Navy) have had a number of articles on USFSPA issues. Thus, there is little excuse for being "totally in the dark" on this subject. If you are like many of your military counterparts, you read the *Times*, or some other contemporary publication to find out what is really happening in the military.

"NIMBY" Syndrome

Next, despite whatever publicity proposed legislation gets, whether it affects the nation as a whole or just your local community, the general tendency is for people to "tune out" or turn their efforts elsewhere once the issue is resolved to their satisfaction. You might call this the NIMBY syndrome—not in my backyard. An example of this was the one major piece of legislation that has been passed since 1982 which addressed the problem of retroactivity of the USFSPA.[5]

Immediately following the enactment of the legislation, the ARA experienced a significant loss of members—presumably those who benefited from the passage of this amendment. Unfortunately, the subject of retroactivity is just one of several equity issues that need to be looked at in terms of reforming the USFSPA. Retirees should consider that without strength in numbers, and continued efforts to work for reform for the benefit of all, not just a few, that any new legislation is doomed (this goes for any association you may belong to). Members who cease belonging should remember that others helped to get the retroactivity issue resolved for them; now they would like your support for further changes.

If you believe you are now "safe"—that is, you have ceased making payments in accordance with what you and your attorney believe is the correct interpretation of the 1990 amendment to the USFSPA, you may want to reconsider joining the ARA after reading the following:

> *In a current New Mexico case, a master sergeant and his wife were divorced in 1973, with the divorce decree making no reference to the retired pay. The ex-spouse filed a petition 16 years after the divorce, seeking a partition of the retired pay, and was subsequently awarded 42 percent of it. The sergeant continued making payments for two more years (until November 1992), and filed a petition with the NM courts seeking termination of the USFSPA payments on the basis of the 1990 congressional amendment. In June 1993, New Mexico's Second Judicial District Court, Bernalillo County, ruled against the retired sergeant, reasoning that under New Mexico law, there*

is a "limited reservation of jurisdiction" that is incorporated into every divorce decree issued in New Mexico. As such, New Mexico has ruled that the conditions of the congressional amendment do not apply and can never apply in New Mexico. The retiree must now seek redress in a federal court, which will, no doubt, cost thousands of dollars.

The decision flies in the face of the intent of Congress and is in direct violation of federal law. Unfortunately, there have been similar decisions in California. A similar decision in another New Mexico case is being appealed through the state courts. The *only* way to stop the state courts from ignoring the federal law is for the federal courts to uphold the supremacy clause of the U.S. Constitution in this context.

Ignorance or Apathy?

The leadership at ARA notes that publicity surrounding the USFSPA, the military retiree, and former spouses, has been out there frequently, albeit not always making headline news. Retiree newsletters published by each of the services have addressed the issue; former spouses' groups have had their stories published in military and local newspapers; various publications[6] cover the subject, including SBP; and the veterans' organizations have devoted some attention to it as well. ARA's membership is less than three-tenths of 1 percent of the nation's USFSPA victims. Yet, single votes have turned the tide in many a law.

Ignorance and apathy do not apply only to the members or nonmembers of associations. Indeed, at the April 1990 hearings for reform of the USFSPA, the senior military leader (a flag officer) who testified was unaware that many reservists are not in paid billets and, therefore, do not receive money in return for their military duty (e.g., on the weekend). When questioned as to whether he had any reservists on his staff or whether any reservists had any substantive input to the law, relative to its inequity with regard to reservists, he said no. Why didn't he know that some reservists are not paid—he was on active duty at the time? Here was a law that significantly affected reservists, in some ways quite differently from the active duty personnel who retire in their late thirties, forties, or early fifties.

The Military Member Is Not the Lone Ranger . . .

The ARA is engaged in continuous dialogue on Capitol Hill and in the Pentagon. In efforts to come to a friendly meeting ground, ARA has also had discussions with EX-POSE.[7]

The Military Coalition[8] has established a subcommittee for USFSPA reform. ARA is coordinating its efforts with the Coalition's. A key factor in the passage of any legislation is, first, DoD approval of the proposed law, and then White House approval of that.

With each election, new faces appear in the House,[9] where proposed legislation is first introduced in subcommittee. Through your membership in an organization like ARA, you can be kept informed. Use that information by contacting *your* congressmen and women and telling them what you want done about the situation, asking them what they are doing about it, and asking their position on it.

What You Can Do

1. Keep yourself informed on USFSPA issues by becoming a member of at least one veterans' organization

that is keeping up in this area. By doing so you will be alerted when you need to shake up Congress with a letter.

2. Find out what position your elected representatives in Congress are taking on this or any other issue important to you. Be sure to let them know you will be keeping track of their interest and voting record regarding the military retiree. Keep in mind that your objective—sustaining benefits for the military retiree—is not the same as your congressmen's and women's, which is getting reelected.

3. Keep the heat on all the veterans' organizations of which you are a member. Find out where they stand on the USFSPA reform and what they are doing about it. Pressure them to press forward with some USFSPA initiatives of their own on Capitol Hill and cooperate with, and assist, the ARA with its legislative program.

4. By all means, become a member of the ARA, actively participate in its activities, and financially support its operations.

5. NEVER GIVE UP!

CHAPTER ENDNOTES

1. An example of the rules and procedures would be the specific service rules that are cited in the *Code of Federal Regulations (C.F.R.)*. The particular process that the services follow with regard to processing USFSPA direct payments may be found in 32 C.F.R. §63. If you are interested in reading the original notice that was published in the *Federal Register*, look up 50 Fed.Reg. 2665 (1985). The procedures for processing child support and alimony are found in 5 C.F.R. §581.

2. It is not the authors' intent to turn this book into a legislative history of the USFSPA. However, for those who would like to read some of the testimony that was presented by the House of Representatives, including that by Rep. Patricia Schroeder (D-

CO), you should consult the following in the *Congressional Record*: H.R. 6030—the debate on USFSPA—as found in 128 Cong.Rec. H4717 (daily ed. July 28, 1982) (reprinted in 1982 U.S. CODE CONG. & ADMIN. NEWS, 1596).

3. See: Rick Maze, "Military leaders mum during debate on COLA CAP," *Air Force Times* (April 19, 1993): 16. This article details why there has been silence among the military leadership regarding the COLA issue.

4. Ibid.

5. Former spouses are now prevented from having a divorce that was finalized before June 26, 1981 reopened to adjudicate the issue of military retired pay, thereby causing retirees to have to pay back retired pay as well as prospective payments. For example, a military member who had been divorced for 15 years, remarried, and retired, could (and did in many cases) find himself facing a judgment for back retired pay plus half of all prospective retired pay. Some in this situation were forced into bankruptcy because the state courts applied this law retroactively.

6. An example of such a publication is the *Retired Military Almanac*, published annually by the Uniformed Services Almanac, Inc., P.O. Box 4144, Falls Church, Virginia 22044. Telephone: (703) 532-1631. See Appendix N for other publications.

7. EX-POSE, the acronym for Ex-Partners of Servicemen (women) for Equality, is an organization primarily of women who are divorced from military members. EX-POSE was approached to provide a "counterpoint" chapter for this book, giving their perspective on the issues; they declined.

8. See Appendix J for a listing of the Coalition's member organizations.

9. See Appendix K on how to write your elected representatives effectively.

APPENDIX A

THE UNIFORMED SERVICES FORMER SPOUSES' PROTECTION ACT

PUBLIC LAW 97-252
Title 10 U.S.C.

1408. Payment of retired or retainer pay in compliance with court orders

(a)   Definitions. - In this section:

(1) The term "Court" means-

(A) any court of competent jurisdiction of any State, the District of Columbia, the Commonwealth of Puerto Rico, Guam, American Samoa, the Virgin Islands, the Northern Mariana Islands, and the Trust Territory of the Pacific Islands;

(B) any court of the United States (as defined in section 451 of title 28) having competent jurisdiction; and

(C) any court of competent jurisdiction of a foreign country with which The United States has an agreement requiring the United States to honor any court order of such country.

(2) The term "court order" means a final decree of divorce, dissolution, annulment, or legal separation issued by a court, or a court ordered, ratified, or approved property settlement incident to such a decree (including a final decree modifying the terms of a previously issued decree of divorce, dissolution, annulment, or legal separation, or a court ordered, ratified, or approved property settlement incident to such previously issued decree), which-

(A) is issued in accordance with the laws of the jurisdiction of that court;

(B) provides for-

(i) payment of child support (as defined in section 462(b) of the Social Security Act (42 U.S.C. 662(b)));

(ii) payment of alimony (as defined in section 462(c) of the Social Security Act (42 U.S.C. 662(c))); or

(iii) division of property (including a division of community property); and

(C) in the case of a division of property, specifically provides for the payment of an amount, expressed in dollars or as a percentage of disposable retired pay, from the disposable retired pay of a member to the spouse or former spouse of that member.

(3) The term "final decree" means a decree from which no appeal may be taken or from which no appeal has been taken within the time allowed for taking such appeals under the laws applicable to such appeals, or a decree from which timely appeal has been taken and such appeal has been finally decided under the laws applicable to such appeals.

(4) The term "disposable retired pay" means the total monthly retired pay to which a member is entitled less amounts which-

(A) are owed by that member to the United States for previous overpayments of retired pay and for recoupments required by law resulting from entitlement to retired pay;

(B) are deducted from the retired pay of such member as a result of forfeitures of retired pay ordered by a court-marital or as a result of a waiver of retired pay required by law in order to receive compensation under title 5 or title 38;

(C) in the case of a member entitled to retired pay under chapter 61 of this title, are equal to the amount of retired pay of the member under that chapter computed using the percentage of the member's disability on the date when the member was retired (or the date on which the member's name was placed on the temporary disability retired list); or

(D) are deducted because of an election under chapter 73 of this title to provide an annuity to a spouse or former spouse to whom payment of a portion of such member's retired pay is being made pursuant to a court order under this section.

(5) The term "member" includes a former member entitled to retired pay under section 1331 of this title.

(6) The term "spouse or former spouse" means the husband or wife, or former husband or wife, respectively, of a member who, on or before the date of a court order, was married to that member.

(7) The term "retired pay" includes retainer pay.

(b) Effective service of process. - For the purposes of this section-

(1) service of a court order is effective if-

(A) an appropriate agent of the Secretary concerned designated for receipt of service of court orders under regulations prescribed pursuant to subsection (h) or, if no agent has been so designated, the Secretary concerned, is personally served or is served by certified or registered mail, return receipt requested;

(B) the court order is regular on its face;

(C) the court order or other documents served with the court order identify the member concerned and include, if possible, the social security number of such member; and

(D) the court order or other documents served with the court order certify that the rights of the member under the Soldiers' and Sailors' Civil Relief Act of 1940 (50 U.S.C. App. 501 et seq.) were observed; and

(2) a court order is regular on its face if the order-

(A) is issued by a court of competent jurisdiction;

(B) is legal in form; and

(C) includes nothing on its face that provides reasonable notice that it is issued without authority of law.

(c) Authority for court to treat retired pay as property of the member and spouse.-

(1) Subject to the limitations of this section, a court may treat disposable retired pay payable to a member for pay periods beginning after June 25, 1981, either as property solely of the member or as property of the member and his spouse in accordance with the law of the jurisdiction of such court. A court may not treat retired pay as property in any proceeding to divide or partition any amount of retired pay of a member as the property of the member and the member's spouse or former spouse if a final decree of divorce, dissolution, annulment, or legal separation (including a court ordered, ratified, or approved property settlement incident to such decree) affecting the member and the member's spouse or former spouse (A) was issued before June 25, 1981, and (B) did not treat (or reserve jurisdiction to treat) any amount of retired pay of the member as property of the member and the member's spouse or former spouse.

(2) Notwithstanding any other provision of law, this section does not create any right, title, or interest which can be sold, assigned, transferred, or otherwise disposed of (including by inheritance) by a spouse or former spouse. Payments by the Secretary concerned under subsection (d) to a spouse or former spouse with respect to a division of retired pay as the property of a member and the member's spouse under this subsection may not be treated as amounts received as retired pay for service in the uniformed services.

(3) This section does not authorize any court to order a member to apply for retirement or retire at a particular time in order to effectuate any payment under this section.

(4) A court may not treat the disposable retired pay of a member in the manner described in paragraph (1) unless the court has jurisdiction over the member by reason of (A) his residence, other than because of military assignment, in the territorial jurisdiction of the court, (B) his domicile in the territorial jurisdiction of the court, or (C) his consent to the jurisdiction of the court.

(d) Payment by the Secretary concerned to spouse or former spouse.-

(1) After effective service on the Secretary concerned of a court order providing for the payment of child support or alimony or, with respect to a division of property, specifically providing for the payment of an amount of the disposable retired pay from a member to the spouse or a former spouse of the member, the Secretary shall make payments (subject to the limitations of this section) from the disposable retired pay of the member to the spouse or former spouse

in an amount sufficient to satisfy the amount of child support and alimony set forth in the court order and, with respect to a division of property, in the amount of disposable retired pay specifically provided for in the court order. In the case of a member entitled to receive retired pay on the date of the effective service of the court order, such payments shall begin not later than 90 days after the date of effective service. In the case of a member not entitled to receive retired pay on the date of the effective service of the court order, such payments shall begin not later than 90 days after the date on which the member first becomes entitled to receive retired pay.

(2) If the spouse or former spouse to whom payments are to be made under this section was not married to the member for a period of 10 years or more during which the member performed at least 10 years of service creditable in determining the member's eligibility for retired pay, payments may not be made under this section to the extent that they include an amount resulting from the treatment by the court under subsection (c) of disposable retired pay of the member as property of the member or property of the member and his spouse.

(3) Payments under this section shall not be made more frequently than once each month, and the Secretary concerned shall not be required to vary normal pay and disbursement cycles for retired or retainer pay in order to comply with a court order.

(4) Payments from the disposable retired pay of a member pursuant to this section shall terminate in accordance with the terms of the applicable court order, but not later than the date of the death of the member or the date of the death of the spouse or former spouse to whom payments are being made, whichever occurs first.

(5) If a court order described in paragraph (1) provides for a division of property (including a division of community property) in addition to an amount of child support or alimony or the payment of an amount of disposable retired pay as the result of the court's treatment of such pay under subsection (c) as property of the member and his spouse, the Secretary concerned shall pay (subject to the limitations of this section) from the disposable retired pay of the member to the spouse or former spouse of the member, any part of the amount payable to the spouse or former spouse under the division of property upon effective service of a final court order of garnishment of such amount from such retired pay.

(e) Limitations.-

(1) The total amount of the disposable retired pay of a mem-

ber payable under all court orders pursuant to subsection (c) may not exceed 50 percent of such disposable retired pay.

(2) In the event of effective service of more than one court order which provide for payment to a spouse and one or more former spouses or to more than one former spouse, the disposable retired pay of the member shall be used to satisfy (subject to the limitations of paragraph (1)) such court orders on a first-come, first-served basis. Such court orders shall be satisfied (subject to the limitations of paragraph (1)) out of that amount of disposable retired pay which remains after the satisfaction of all court orders which have been previously served.

(3)(A) In the event of effective service of conflicting court orders under this section which assert to direct that different amounts be paid during a month to the same spouse or former spouse of the same member, the Secretary concerned shall-

(i) pay to that spouse from the member's disposable retired pay the least amount directed to be paid during that month by any such conflicting court order, but not more than the amount of disposable retired pay which remains available for payment of such court orders based on when such court orders were effectively served and the limitations of paragraph (1) and subparagraph (B) of paragraph (4);

(ii) retain an amount of disposable retired pay that is equal to the lesser of-

(I) the difference between the largest amount required by any conflicting court order to be paid to the spouse or former spouse and the amount payable to the spouse or former spouse under clause (i); and

(II) the amount of disposable retired pay which remains available for payment of any conflicting court order based on when such court order was effectively served and the limitations of paragraph (1) and subparagraph (B) of paragraph (4); and

(iii) pay to that member the amount which is equal to the amount of that member's disposable retired pay (less any amount paid during such month pursuant to legal process served under section 459 of the Social Security Act (42 U.S.C. 659) and any amount paid during such month pursuant to court orders effectively served under this section, other than such conflicting court orders) minus-

(I) the amount of disposable retired pay paid under clause (i); and

(II) the amount of disposable retired pay retained under clause (ii).

(B) The Secretary concerned shall hold the amount retained under clause (ii) of subparagraph (a) until such time as that Secretary is provided with a court order which has been certified by the member and the spouse or former spouse to be valid and applicable to the retained amount. Upon being provided with such an order, the Secretary shall pay the retained amount in accordance with the order.

(4)(A) In the event of effective service of a court order under this section and the service of legal process pursuant to section 459 of the Social Security Act (42 U.S.C. 659), both of which provide for payments during a month from the same member, satisfaction of such court orders and legal process from the retired pay of the member shall be on a first-come, first-served basis. Such court orders and legal process shall be satisfied out of moneys which are subject to such orders and legal process and which remain available in accordance with the limitations of paragraph (1) and subparagraph (B) of this paragraph during such month after the satisfaction of all court orders or legal process which have been previously served.

(B) Notwithstanding any other provision of law, the total amount of the disposable retired pay of a member payable by the Secretary concerned under all court orders pursuant to this section and all legal processes pursuant to section 459 of the Social Security Act (42 U.S.C. 659) with respect to a member may not exceed 65 percent of the amount of the retired pay payable to such member that is considered under section 462 of the Social Security Act (42 U.S.C. 662) to be remuneration for employment that is payable by the United States.

(5) A court order which itself or because of previously served court orders provides for the payment of an amount which exceeds the amount of disposable retired pay available for payment because of the limit set forth in paragraph (1), or which, because of previously served court orders or legal process previously served under section 459 of the Social Security Act (42 U.S.C. 659), provides for payment of an amount that exceeds the maximum amount permitted under paragraph (1) or subparagraph (B) of paragraph (4), shall not be considered to be irregular on its face solely for that reason. However, such order shall be considered to be fully satisfied for purposes of this section by the payment to the spouse or former spouse of the maximum amount of disposable retired pay permitted under paragraph (1) and subparagraph (B) of paragraph (4).

(6) Nothing in this section shall be construed to relieve a member of liability for the payment of alimony, child support, or other payments required by a court order on the grounds that payments made out of disposable retired pay under this section have been made in the maximum amount permitted under paragraph (1) or subparagraph (B) of paragraph (4). Any such unsatisfied obligation of a member may be enforced by any means available under law other than the means provided under this section in any case in which the maximum amount permitted under paragraph (1) has been paid and under section 459 of the Social Security Act (42 U.S.C. 659) in any case in which the maximum amount permitted under subparagraph (B) of paragraph (4) has been paid.

(f) Immunity of officers and employees of United States.-

(1) The United States and any officer or employee of the United States shall not be liable with respect to any payment made from retired pay to any member, spouse, or former spouse pursuant to a court order that is regular on its face if such payment is made in accordance with this section and the regulations prescribed pursuant to subsection (h).

(2) An officer or employee of the United States who, under regulations prescribed pursuant to subsection (h), has the duty to respond to interrogatories shall not be subject under any law to any disciplinary action or civil or criminal liability or penalty for, or because of, any disclosure of information made by him in carrying out any of his duties which directly or indirectly pertain to answering such interrogatories.

(g) Notice to member of service of court order on Secretary concerned.- A person receiving effective service of a court order under this section shall, as soon as possible, but not later than 30 days after the date on which effective service is made, send a written notice of such court order (together with a copy of such order) to the member affected by the court order at his last known address.

(h) Benefits for dependents who are victims of abuse by members losing right to retired pay.-

(1) If, in the case of a member or former member of the armed forces referred to in paragraph (2)(A), a court order provides (in the manner applicable to a division of property) for the payment of an amount from the disposable retired pay of that member or former member (as certified under paragraph (4)) to an eligible spouse or former spouse of that member or former member, the Secretary con-

cerned, beginning upon effective service of such court order, shall pay that amount in accordance with this subsection to such spouse or former spouse.

(2) A spouse or former spouse of a member or former member of the armed forces is eligible to receive payment under this subsection if-

(A) the member or former member, while a member of the armed forces and after becoming eligible to be retired from the armed forces on the basis of years of service, has eligibility to receive retired pay terminated as a result of misconduct while a member involving abuse of a spouse or dependent child (as defined in regulations prescribed by the Secretary of Defense); and

(B) the spouse or former spouse-

(i) was the victim of the abuse and was married to the member or former member at the time of that abuse; or

(ii) is a natural or adopted parent of a dependent child of the member or former member who was the victim of the abuse.

(3) The amount certified by the Secretary concerned under paragraph (4) with respect to a member or former member of the armed forces referred to in paragraph (2)(A) shall be deemed to be the disposable retired pay of that member or former member for the purposes of this subsection.

(4) Upon the request of a court or an eligible spouse or former spouse of a member or former member of the armed forces referred to in paragraph (2)(A) in connection with a civil action for the issuance of a court order in the case of that member or former member, the Secretary concerned shall determine and certify the amount of the monthly retired pay that the member or former member would have been entitled to receive as of the date of the certification-

(A) if the member or former member's eligibility for retired pay had not been terminated as described in paragraph (2)(A); and

(B) if, in the case of a member or former member not in receipt of retired pay immediately before that termination of eligibility for retired pay, the member or former member had retired on the effective date of that termination eligibility.

(5) A court order under this subsection may provide that whenever retired pay is increased under section 1401a of this title (or any other provision of law), the amount payable under the court order to the spouse or former spouse of a member or former member described in paragraph (2)(A) shall be increased at the same time by the percent by which the retired pay of the member or former member would have been increased if the member or former member were receiving retired pay.

(6) Notwithstanding any other provision of law, a member or former member of the armed forces referred to in paragraph (2)(A) shall have no ownership interest in, or claim against, any amount payable under this section to a spouse or former spouse of the member or former member.

(7)(A) If a former spouse receiving payments under this subsection with respect to a member or former member referred to in paragraph (2)(A) marries again after such payments begin, the eligibility of the former spouse to receive further payments under this subsection shall terminate on the date of such marriage.

(B) A person's eligibility to receive payments under this subsection that is terminated under subparagraph (A) by reason of remarriage shall be resumed in the event of the termination of that marriage by the death of that person's spouse or by annulment or divorce. The resumption of payments shall begin as of the first day of the month in which that marriage is so terminated. The monthly amount of the payments shall be the amount that would have been paid if the continuity of the payments had not been interrupted by the marriage.

(8) Payments in accordance with this subsection shall be made out of funds in the Department of Defense Military Retirement Fund established by section 1461 of this title.

(9)(A) A spouse or former spouse of a member or former member of the armed forces referred to paragraph (2)(A), while receiving payments in accordance with this subsection, shall be entitled to receive medical and dental care, to use commissary and exchange stores, and to receive any other benefit that a spouse or a former spouse of a retired member of the armed forces is entitled to receive on the basis of being a spouse or former spouse, as the case may be, of a retired member of the armed forces in the same manner as if the member or former member referred to in paragraph (2)(A) was entitled to retired pay.

(B) A dependent child of a member or former member referred

to in paragraph (2)(A) who was a member of the household of the member or former member at the time of the misconduct described in paragraph (2)(A) shall be entitled to receive medical and dental care, to use commissary and exchange stores, and to have other benefits provided to dependents of retired members of the armed forces in the same manner as if the member or former member referred to in paragraph (2)(A) was entitled to retired pay.

(C) If a spouse or former spouse or a dependent child eligible or entitled to receive a particular benefit under this paragraph is eligible or entitled to receive that benefit under another provision of law, the eligibility or entitlement of that spouse or former spouse or dependent child to such benefit shall be determined under such other provisions of law instead of this paragraph.

(10) In this subsection, the term "dependent child," with respect to a member or former member of the armed forces referred to in paragraph (2)(A), means an unmarried legitimate child, including an adopted child or a stepchild of the member of former member, who-

(A) is under 18 years of age;

(B) is incapable of self-support because of a mental or physical incapacity that existed before becoming 18 years of age and is dependent on the member or former member for over one-half of the child's support; or

(C) if enrolled in a full-time course of study in an institution of higher education recognized by the Secretary of Defense for the purposes of this subparagraph, is under 23 years of age and is dependent on the member or former member for over one-half of the child's support.

(i) Regulations.- The Secretaries concerned shall prescribe uniform regulations for the administration of this section.

(As amended Pub.L. 98-525, Title VI, Sec. 643(a)-(d), Oct. 19, 1984, 98 Stat. 2547, 2548; Pub.L. 99-661, Div. A, Title VI, Sec. 644(a), Nov. 14, 1986, 100 Stat. 3887; Pub.L. 100-26 Sec. 3(3), Apr. 21, 1987, 101 Stat. 278; Pub.L. 100-26, Sec. 7(h)(1), Apr. 21, 1987, 101 Stat. 282; Pub.L. 101-189, Div. A, Title VI, Sec. 658(a)(5), Title XVI, Sec. 1622(e)(6), Nov. 29, 1989, 103 Stat. 1462, 1605; Pub.L. 101-510, Div. A, Title V, Sec. 555(a)-(d), (f), (g), Nov. 5, 1990, 104 Stat. 1569, 1570; Pub.L. 102-190, Div. A, Title X Sec. 1061(a)(7), Dec. 5 1991, 105 Stat. 1472; Pub.L. 102-484, Div. A, Title VI, Sec. 653(a), Oct. 28, 1992, 106 Stat. 2426.)

APPENDIX B

McCarty v. McCarty, 1981

Extract From *The Supreme Court Reporter*

REFERENCE: 453 U.S. 210, 69 L.Ed.2d 589

Richard John McCARTY, Appellant

v.

Patricia Ann McCARTY.

No. 80-5.

Argued March 2, 1981.

Decided June 26, 1981.

A California Court of Appeal, First Appellate District, affirmed an award by a superior court to a wife on dissolution of marriage. On appeal, the Supreme Court, Justice Blackmun, held that, on dissolution of the marriage, federal law precludes a state court from dividing military nondisability retired pay pursuant to state community property laws.

Justice Rehnquist dissented and filed opinion in which Justice Brennan and Justice Stewart joined.

Syllabus*

A regular commissioned officer of the United States Army who retires after 20 years of service is entitled to retired pay. Retired pay terminates with the officer's death, although he may designate a beneficiary to receive any arrearages that remain unpaid at death. In addition there are statutory plans that allow the officer to set aside a portion of his retired pay for his survivors. Appellant, a Regular Army

Colonel, filed a petition in California Superior Court for dissolution of his marriage to appellee. At the time, he had served approximately 18 of the 20 years required for retirement with pay. Under California law, each spouse, upon dissolution of a marriage, has an equal and absolute right to a half interest in all community and quasi-community property, but retains his or her separate property. In his petition, appellant requested, inter alia, that his military retirement benefits be confirmed to him as his separate property. The Superior Court held, however, that such benefits were subject to division as quasi-community property, and accordingly ordered appellant to pay to appellee a specified portion of the benefits upon retirement. Subsequently, appellant retired and began receiving retired pay; under the dissolution decree, appellee was entitled to approximately 45% of the retired pay. On review of this award, the California Court of Appeal affirmed, rejecting appellant's contention that because the federal scheme of military retirement benefits preempts state community property law, the Supremacy Clause precluded the trial court from awarding appellee a portion of his retired pay.

Held: Federal law precludes a state court from dividing military retired pay pursuant to state community property laws.

(a) There is a conflict between the terms of the federal military retirement statutes and the community property right asserted by appellee. The military retirement system confers no entitlement to retired pay upon the retired member's spouse, and does not embody even a limited "community property concept." Rather, the language, structure, and history of the statutes make it clear that retired pay continues to be the personal entitlement of the retiree.

(b) Moreover, the application of community property principles to military retired pay threatens grave harm to "clear and substantial" federal interests. Thus, the community property division of retired pay, by reducing the amounts that Congress has determined are necessary for the retired member, has the potential to frustrate the congressional objective of providing for the retired service member. In addition, such a division has the potential to interfere with the congressional goals of having the military retirement system serve as an inducement for enlistment and re-enlistment and as an encouragement to orderly promotion and a youthful military.

---

*The syllabus constitutes no part of the opinion of the Court but has been prepared by the Reporter of Decisions for the convenience of the reader.

APPENDIX C

Mansell Decision on Disability Retirement

Mansell v. Mansell, 1989
Extract From *The Supreme Court Reporter*
REFERENCE: 490 U.S. 581, 104 L.Ed.2d 675

Gerald E. MANSELL, Appellant
v.
Gaye M. MANSELL.
No. 87-201

Argued January 10, 1989.
Decided May 30, 1989.

Former husband sought modification of divorce decree by removing the provision that required him to share his total retirement pay with his former wife. The California Superior Court, Merced County, denied the request without opinion. Former husband appealed. The California Court of Appeal affirmed. The California Supreme Court denied the former husband's petition for review. Appeal was taken. The Supreme Court, Justice Marshall, held that military retirement pay that had been waived by the former husband in order to receive veterans' disability benefits was not community property divisible upon divorce.

Syllabus*

In direct response to *McCarty v. McCarty,* 453 U.S. 210, 101 S.Ct. 2728, 69 L.Ed.2d 589, which held that federal law as it then existed completely pre-empted the application of state community property law to military retirement pay, Congress enacted the Uniformed Services Former Spouses' Protection Act (Act), 10 U.S.C. Sec. 1408 (1982 ed. and Supp. V), which authorizes state courts to treat as community property "disposable retired or retainer pay," 10 U.S.C. Sec. 1408(c)(1), specifically defining such pay to exclude, inter alia, any military retirement pay waived in order for the retiree to receive veterans' disability benefits, 10 U.S.C. Sec. 1408(a)(4)(B). The Act also creates a mechanism whereby the Federal Government will make direct community property payments of up to 50 percent of disposable retired or retainer pay to certain former spouses who present state-court orders granting such pay. A pre-*McCarty* property settlement agreement between appellant and appellee, who were divorced in a county Superior Court in California, a community property State, provided that appellant would pay appellee 50 percent of his total military retirement pay, including that portion of such pay which he had waived in order to receive military disability benefits. After the Act's passage, the Superior Court denied appellant's request to modify the divorce decree by removing the provision requiring him to share his total retirement pay with appellee. The State Court of Appeal affirmed, rejecting appellant's contention that the Act precluded the lower court from treating as community property the military retirement pay appellant had waived to receive disability benefits. In so holding, the court relied on a State Supreme Court decision which reasoned that the Act did not limit a state court's ability to treat total military retirement pay as community property and to enforce a former spouse's rights to such pay through remedies other than direct Federal Government payments.

Held: The Act does not grant state courts the power to treat as property divisible upon divorce military retirement pay waived by the retiree in order to receive veterans' disability benefits. In light of 10 U.S.C. Sec. 1408(a)(4)(B)'s limiting language as to such waived pay, the Act's plain and precise language establishes that 10 U.S.C. Sec. 1408(c)(1) grants state courts the authority to treat only disposable retired pay, not total retired pay, as community property. Appellee's argument that the Act has no preemptive effect of its own and must be read as a garnishment statute designed solely to limit when the Federal Government will make direct payments to a former spouse, and that, accordingly, 10 U.S.C. Sec. 1408(a)(4)(B) defines "disposable retired or retainer pay" only because payments under the statutory direct payment mechanism are limited to amounts defined by that term, is flawed for two reasons. First, the argument completely ignores the fact that 10 U.S.C. Sec. 1408(c)(1) also uses the quoted phrase to limit specifically and plainly the extent to which state courts may treat military retirement pay as community property. Second, each of 10 U.S.C. Sec. 1408(c)'s other subsections imposes new substantive limits on state courts' power to divide military retirement pay, and it is unlikely that all of the section, except for 10 U.S.C. Sec. 1408(c)(1), was intended to pre-empt state law. Thus, the garnishment argument misplaces its reliance on the fact that the Act's saving clause expressly contemplates that a retiree will be liable for "other payments" in excess of those made under the direct payment mechanism, since that clause is more plausibly interpreted as serving the limited purpose of defeating any inference that the mechanism displaced state courts' authority to divide and garnish property not covered by the mechanism. Appellee's contention that giving effect to the plain and precise statutory language would thwart the Act's obvious purposes of rejecting McCarty and restoring to state courts their pre-*McCarty* authority is not supported by the legislative history, which, read as a whole, indicates that Congress intended both to create new benefits for former spouses and to place on state courts limits designed to protect military retirees.

Reversed and remanded.

MARSHALL, J., delivered the opinion of the Court, in which REHNQUIST, C.J., and BRENNAN, WHITE, STEVENS, SCALLA and KENNEDY, J.J., joined. O'CONNOR, J., filed a dissenting opinion, in which BLACKMUN, J., joined.

---

*The syllabus constitutes no part of the opinion of the Court but has been prepared by the Reporter of Decisions for the convenience of the reader.

Additional Citations

> *Mansell v. Mansell (Forbes)*, 109 S. Ct. 2023 (1989), 104 L.Ed.2d 675 (1989), 57 U.S.L.W. 4567, 10 E.B.C. 2521. On remand *In re Marriage of Mansell* (1989, 5th Dist) 216 Cal.App.3d 937, 265 Cal.Rptr.227, 1989 Cal.App; 217 Cal.App.3d 319, 1989 Cal.App. (Prior history: 487 U.S. 1217, 101 L.Ed.2d 904, 108 S.Ct. 2868)

APPENDIX D

Barker v. Kansas

Barker v. Kansas

SUPREME COURT OF THE UNITED STATES
No. 91-611

KEYTON E. BARKER AND PAULINE BARKER,
ET AL.,
PETITIONERS v. KANSAS ET AL.

ON WRIT OF CERTIORARI TO THE SUPREME
COURT OF KANSAS
(April 21, 1992)

JUSTICE WHITE delivered the
opinion of the Court.

The State of Kansas taxes the benefits received from the United States by military retirees but does not tax the benefits received by retired state and local government employees. Kan. Stat. Ann. Sec. 79-3201 et seq. (1989).[1] The issue before us is whether the tax imposed on the military retirees is inconsistent with 4 U.S.C. Sec. 111, which provides:

"The United States consents to the taxation of pay or compensation for personal service as an officer or employee of the United States, a territory or possession or political subdivision thereof, the government of the district of Columbia, or an agency or instrumentality of one or more of the foregoing, by a duly constituted taxing authority having jurisdiction, if the taxation does not discriminate against the officer or employee because of the source of the pay or compensation."

[1]As the Kansas Supreme Court explained, to arrive at the adjusted gross income of a taxpayer under the Kansas Income Tax Act, the starting point is the adjusted gross income under the federal Internal Revenue Code, which includes retirement benefits received by retired military officials and state and local government retirees. 249 Kan. 186, 190-101, 815 P. 2d 46, 49-50 (1991). As relevant for present purposes, in calculating Kansas' adjusted gross income, the retirement benefits of state and local governments are deducted and are exempt from taxation. See Kan. Stat.Ann. Sec. 79-32,117(c)(ii)(Supp. 1990); Sec. 74-4923(b) (Supp. 1990); see also 249 Kan., at 190-191, 815 P. 2d, at 49-50 (listing classes exempt from state taxation). Benefits received under the Federal Civil Service Retirement System and by retired railroad employees are also exempt. Kan.Stat.Ann. Sections 79-32, 117(c)(vii) and (viii) (Supp. 1990). Not deducted and hence taxable are benefits received by retired military personnel, certain CIA employees, officials serving in the National Oceanic and Atmospheric Association or the Public Health Service, and by retired federal judges. See 249 Kan., at 205, 815 P. 2d, at 58.

Syllabus*
BARKER ET AL. v. KANSAS ET AL.
CERTIORARI TO THE SUPREME COURT OF KANSAS
No. 91-611. Argued March 3, 1992--Decided April 21, 1992

Title 4 U.S.C. Sec. 111 authorizes the States to tax federal employees' compensation if the taxation does not discriminate against the employees because of the compensation's source. After Davis v. Michigan Dept. of Treasury, 489 U.S. 803, invalidated, under Sec. 111 and the doctrine of intergovernmental tax immunity, the Michigan income tax imposed on the benefits of federal, but not state and local, civil service retirees, petitioners filed suit in a Kansas state court challenging that State's imposition of an income tax on federal military retirement benefits but not on the benefits received by retired state and local government employees. In affirming the trial court's grant of summary judgment for the state defendants, the State Supreme Court concluded that military retirement benefits constitute reduced pay for reduced current services, in contrast to the deferred compensation for past services embodied in state and local government retirement benefits, and that this "significant difference" justified the State's differential treatment of the two classes of retirees under Davis, supra, at 816.

Held: The Kansas tax on military retirees is inconsistent with Sec. 111. The State Supreme Court's conclusion that, for purposes of state taxation, military retirement benefits may be characterized as current compensation for reduced current services does not survive analysis on several bases. First, there are no "significant differences" between military retirees and state and local government retirees in terms of calculating retirement benefits. The amount of retired pay a service member receives is computed not on the basis of the continuing duties he actually performs, but on the basis of years served on active duty and the rank obtained prior to retirement. Military benefits thus are determined in a manner very similar to that of the Kansas Public Employee Retirement System. Second, this Court's precedents discussing military retirement pay provide no support for the state court's holding. The statement in *United States v. Tyler*, 105 U.S. 244, 245, that such pay is effectively indistinguishable from current compensation at a reduced rate was made in the context of the particular holding of that case, and cannot be taken as establishing that retirement benefits are for all purposes the equivalent of current compensation for reduced current services. And, although *McCarty v. McCarty*, 453 U.S. 210, 222, referred to *Tyler*, it did not expressly approve *Tyler's* description of military retirement pay, but specifically reserved the question whether federal law prohibits a State from characterizing such pay as deferred compensation and urged the States to tread with caution in this area. Third, an examination of other federal statutes treating military retirement pay indicates that Congress for many purposes does not consider such pay to be current compensation for reduced current services. See, e.g., 10 U.S.C. Sec. 1408(c)(1); 26 U.S.C. Sec. 219(f)(1). Thus, military retirement benefits, like the benefits paid to Kansas government retirees, are to be considered deferred pay for past services for purposes of Sec. 111. Pp. 3-10.

249 Kan. 186, 815 P. 2d 46, reversed and remanded.

WHITE, J., delivered the opinion for a unanimous Court. STEVENS, J., filed a concurring opinion, in which THOMAS, J., joined.

---

*The syllabus constitutes no part of the opinion of the Court but has been prepared by the Reporter of Decisions for the convenience of the reader.

APPENDIX E

UNJUST TAKING CASE

**United States Court of Appeals
for the Federal Circuit**

"UNJUST TAKING" CASE
89-1106

ALBERT JOHN FERN, JR., JOHN T. FLANNAGAN,
ROBERT JEFFREY, DONNALD KIPPENHAVER,
JAMES H. POWELL, ROBERT LOUIS STIRM, MAX E.
THOMPSON,
JACK TRAHAN AND DAVID E. WALENTOWSKI,
Plaintiffs-Appellants,

v.

THE UNITED STATES,
Defendant-Appellee.

DECIDED: July 16, 1990

Before NIES, Chief Judge* NEWMAN and ARCHER,
Circuit Judges. NIES, Chief Judge.

This appeal is from the final judgment of the United States Claims
Court, *Fern v. United States*, 15 Cl. Ct. 580 (1988) (Lydon, J.), dis-
missing a complaint which sought just compensation under the Fifth

Amendment to the United States Constitution arising from or as a result of the enactment of the Uniform Services Former Spouses' Protection Act, Pub. L. No. 97-252, 96 Stat. 718 (1985) (codified at 10 U.S.C. Sec. 1408(c)(1)(1988)) (hereinafter "the Act" or "FSPA"). appellants are retired members of the armed forces each of whom receive retired pay by reason of a least 20 years of satisfactory active duty service in the military. Each appellant seeks compensation from the United States for the portion of retired

---

* Chief Judge Nies assumed the position of Chief Judge on June 27, 1990.

---

pay which his former spouse has been awarded pursuant to a divorce decree. Appellants attribute their deprivation of part of their retired pay to the change made by FSPA in federal law. On cross-motions for summary judgment, the Claims Court held that FSPA did not effect a "taking" by the United States of appellants' property for public use within the meaning of the Fifth Amendment. We affirm.

I

Background

This appeal requires consideration of the interplay between the divorce laws of certain community property states and the federal statutes relating to military retired pay. The parties do not distinguish between specific state community property laws and, therefore, we will simply refer to California law.[1]

California treats property acquired during marriage as community property. When a couple divorces in that state, community and quasi-community property is divided equally between the spouses while each spouse retains full ownership of any separate property. In California, pension benefits are deemed property and, to the extent accrued during marriage, such property belongs to both spouses, as community or quasi-community property. California has applied these principles to military retired pay benefits the same as to any pension benefits and, upon divorce, has divided the benefits between the spouses, pro tanto. See McCarty v. McCarty, 453 U.S. 210, 216-18 (1981); In re Marriage of Fithian, 10 Cal. 3d 592, 111 Cal. Rptr. 369, 517 P.2d 449 (en banc), cert. denied, 419 U.S. 825 (1974); cf. Cearley v. Cearley, 544 S.W.2d 661 (Tex. 1976). In Fithian, the Supreme Court of California rejected the argument that, by federal statute, military retired pay had to be treated as the separate property of the retiree notwithstanding that community property laws of a particular state

---

[1] The appellants' divorces were granted under the laws of California, New Mexico, Texas or Washington.

generally required division of pension benefits.   At the same time, Alaska, another state which also treats pension benefits as marital property, took the view that federal law regarding military retired pay did preempt state law, and prevented an award of any part of military retired pay to the ex-spouse of the service member.   See *Cose v. Cose*, 592 P.2d 1230, 1232 (Alaska 1979).   In *McCarty*, the Supreme Court resolved this conflict, holding that the federal statutes then governing military retired pay preempted state law and prevented state courts from treating military retired pay as marital property.

In direct response to the *McCarty* decision, Congress enacted FSPA which, in section 1408(c)(1), authorizes state courts to treat disposable retired pay as property solely of the retiree or as property of the retiree and his spouse. To this extent, the Act removed federal preemption retroactively to June 25, 1981, the day before the *McCarty* decision.   See *Mansell v. Mansell*, 490 U.S. 581, 109 S. Ct. 2033 (1989).

All of the appellants here had received divorce decrees prior to the passage of FSPA. However, appellants classify themselves into three groups: (A) "final-decree" plaintiffs who had received divorce decrees that specifically refused to divide military retired pay with a spouse in view of *McCarty*; (B) "omitted-asset" plaintiffs where the decrees did not refer to retired pay; and (C) "pre-McCarty" plaintiffs whose decrees had divided retired pay, pursuant to a state's community property law, but who had stopped paying after the *McCarty* decision. Former spouses of (A) and (B) class plaintiffs successfully petitioned their respective divorce courts to reopen and modify outstanding final decrees to give them a right to proportionate shares of their husband's benefits. The former spouses of class (C) plaintiffs successfully brought enforcement proceedings on the original decrees after the enactment of FSPA. While there are factual differences between the groups, the differences are not legally significant to the arguments advanced for reversal of the Claims Court and, except where the text indicates otherwise, the same analysis is applied to all claimants. For convenience, we refer to all claimants as "Fern."

Fern's position is that the division of his retired pay benefits, albeit directly resulting from a state court decree, was made possible only by passage of FSPA. In Fern's view, the Act constitutes a taking of his property by the United States for which compensation must be paid under the Fifth Amendment. Fern identifies the "taken property" variously as his interest in the "final judgement" which was reopened because of the Act; "property entitlements of a final judgment"; "fully earned retired pay"; "vested property rights [in the] entirety of his retired pay"; and "impair[ment]" or "alteration of plaintiff's contractual rights" or "entitlements."   The statute is constitutional, per Fern, but the government must pay the cost of the past and future benefits conferred on the former spouses by FSPA, not the retirees. In its simplest terms, Fern asks us to require the government to pay up to a pension and a half.

The government argues that Fern has not established a "taking" by the United States; that the challenged statute merely abrogates federal preemption of state law and allows state courts to apportion military retired pay benefits between spouses; that Fern has no property interest in federal preemption of state law; and that, if the statute were to be construed as directly reducing the amount of Fern's retired pay, Fern has, in any event, no property interest in the level of that pay. Accordingly, the government urges us to uphold the judgment of the Claims Court.

II
Issue

Is the United States required to pay just compensation under the Fifth Amendment to the extent of the economic effect on a retiree personally, resulting from a state court divorce decree following the withdrawal of federal preemption of state community property laws respecting military retired pay?

III
Opinion

The statute with which we are concerned, 10 U.S.C. Sec. 1408(c)(1) (1988) provides specifically in pertinent part:

Subject to the limitations of this section, a court may treat disposable retired or retainer pay payable to a member for pay periods beginning after June 25, 1981, either as property solely of the member or a property of the member and his spouse in accordance with the law of the jurisdiction of such court.

No facile formula is available for making the determination of whether a governmental "taking" of private property for public use has occurred within the meaning of the Fifth Amendment. *Connolly v. Pension Benefit Guar. Corp.*, 475 U.S. 211, 224 (1986). Rather, the Supreme Court stated therein, in connection with alleged takings by statute or regulation, that it "relied instead on ad hoc, factual inquiries into the circumstances of each particular case." Id. (citing *Ruckelshaus v. Monsanto Co.*, 467 U.S. 986, 1005 (1984); *Kaiser Aetna v. United States*, 444 U.S. 164, 175 (1979)). However, the Court "identified three factors which have particular significance in reaching a determination: (1) the economic impact of the [statute] on the claimant; (2) the extent to which the [statute] has interfered with distinct [and reasonable] investment-backed expectations; and (3) the character of the government action." Id. at 224-25 (internal quotation marks omitted). See *Monsanto Co.*, 467 U.S. at 1005; *PruneYard Shopping Center v. Robins*, 447 U.S. 74, 82-83 (1980); *Penn Cent. Transp. Co. v. New York City*, 438 U.S. 104, 124 (1978). As an initial matter, we note that both parties assume that when a statute or regulation does effect a taking without compensation which falls within the proscription of the Fifth Amendment, the remedy is compensation for the taking rather than a declaration that the statute is unconstitutional. Indeed, Fern insists that FSPA is constitutional although it would be unconstitutional, per Fern, if the government does not pay the amount "taken" from him by the divorce decree.

We do not find the case law so clear with respect to when a statute should be voided as violating the constitutional bar and when the availability of a Tucker Act claim would save the statute. Compare ·*Hodel v. Irving*, 481 U.S. 704 (1987), with *Preseault v. ICC*, ___U.S.___, 110 S. Ct. 914,___(1990). The availability of a Tucker Act remedy, here, may not afford the full relief requested by Fern with respect to past and future payments to his wife. It would require a rewriting of the statute to effectuate the system Fern seeks to have implemented, namely payment into the future of Fern's full amount of retired pay to him plus the amount of his ex-spouse's share as an addition thereto. However, in view of our ruling that there has been no taking by the United States, we need not decide whether the future relief Fern seeks would be appropriate.[2]

Before applying the above-quoted *Connolly* guidelines to determine whether a "taking" has occurred, it is necessary to analyze Fern's asserted "property." In effect, Fern argues that part of his military retired pay has been taken by FSPA because the benefits received must be divided with his wife.

---

[2] A computation of a lump sum evaluation of future payments (as an alternative to continuing future payments) would appear nebulous inasmuch as a military member has no entitlement to any continued level of retirement pay. Congress may alter and even eliminate military retired pay benefits whether classified as "current pay for reduced current services" or pension benefits. See *Hisquierdo v. Hisquierdo*, 439 U.S. 572, 575 (1979) (pension benefits); see also *Atkins v. Parker*, 472 U.S. 115, 129-30 & n.32 (1985) (pension benefits); *United States v. Larianoff*, 431 U.S. 864, 879 (1977) (reduction in pay); *Costello v. United States*, 587 F.2d 424, 426 (9th Cir. 1978) (en banc), cert. denied, 442 U.S. 929 (1979) (reduction in pay).

Fern's theory intermixes two separate and distinct bundles of rights-- his right to military retired pay vis-a-vis the government, a matter of federal law, and ownership of assets of a marriage vis-a-vis a former spouse, a matter of state law into a single sheaf.

With respect to Fern's entitlement to retired pay vis-a-vis the government, FSPA had no effect. Fern's "entitlement" against the government remained exactly the same before and after FSPA. Nothing was "taken" or "diminished" from the amount of military retired pay to which he was or may become entitled under federal law. It is immaterial whether such rights are deemed vested statutory rights, purported contractual obligations, or investment-backed expectations: Fern's asserted rights to benefits from the federal government have been fully satisfied and remain intact.

What has been affected by FSPA concerns ownership of military retired pay between Fern and his former spouse. Unless preempted, the laws of the states determine whether such retirement payments must be shared by marriage partners. Under the law of California and the other community property states involved here, individual pension benefits, accrued as a result of a spouse's employment during the marriage, are deemed the property of both spouses equally, to the extent accrued during the marriage. Thus, appellants had no ownership right in the entirety of their military retired pay vis-a-vis their spouses. A spouse, upon divorce, simply was barred from receiving a share of that asset, which the state otherwise would have recognized as her property, by the preemptive effect of the federal law. See *McCarty*, 453 U.S. 210 (1981); see also *Mansell v. Mansell*, U.S. , 109 S. Ct. 2033 (1989) (federal law continues to preempt division of military disability pay).

The lifting of that federal bar did not have the character or effect of a partial transfer of an appellant's military retired pay to his wife by the United States. That occurred only because a particular state in a particular divorce proceeding acted affirmatively to recognize the spouse's right to receive a share of her husband's retired pay as property of the marriage under state law.[3] It is true that Congress expected community property states would be likely to take steps to divide military retired pay between spouses under divorce decrees after enactment of FSPA. However, we cannot agree that the award of benefits to Fern's former spouse by the state became an act of the United States because Congress was aware that the community property states could take this action if Congress lifted the bar of preemption. Nor is the United States the actor with respect to the retroactive application of state law to payments Fern received after June 25, 1981. While allowing state law to be applied retroactively, FSPA itself had no direct effect, retroactive or otherwise, on division of the payments.[4] This decision was left entirely up to each state.

While Fern does not openly assert that he has a property right in continued federal preemption of state law, essentially that is a stick he would have to have in his bundles of rights to bar his former wife from sharing in his military retired pay. Lest there be any question, we reject the idea that continued preemption is a property right either as part of Fern's rights as against the government or his rights as against his wife. cf. *Duke Power Co. v. Carolina Env. Study Group*, 438 U.S. 59, 88 n.32 (1978); *New York Cent. R.R. v. White*, 243 U.S. 188, 197-98 (1917); *Second Employers'*

---

[3] California enacted a special statute to allow reopening of final decrees for this purpose. See Cal. Civ. Code Sec. 5124 (Deering 1984) (repealed by its own terms Jan. 1, 1986).

---

[4] We express no opinion on whether retroactive application of formerly preempted state law constitutes a taking by the state. Indeed, the legal effect of FSPA was not to abrogate completely the ban of federal preemption, but only to lift it as of June 25, 1981. Prior to that date, per *McCarty*, presumably preemption remains in effect.

Liability Cases, 223 U.S. 1, 50 (1911); *Munn v. Illinois*, 94 U.S. 113, 134 (1876) ("a person has no property, no vested interest, in any rule of common law. Rights of property which have been created [by common law] may not be taken away without due process; but the law itself, as a rule of conduct, may be changed at the will or even at the whim, of the legislature, unless prevented by constitutional limitations.").[5]

Summarizing the application of the three pronged test of *Connolly* (and other Supreme Court precedent) to Fern's "property" rights in retired pay, we conclude that the FSPA has no economic impact on Fern's rights to military retired pay vis-a-vis the United States and is at best an indirect cause of the reduction in the amount of retired pay he may keep for himself under his divorce decree. The action of the United States in enacting FSPA was correctly characterized by the Claims Court as a lifting of federal preemption of state law. That is not the kind of action which falls within the concepts of a "taking" of property.

IV
Conclusion

For the foregoing reasons, we hold that the United States has not taken Fern's property by enactment of FSPA. Accordingly, the judgment of the United States Claims Court is AFFIRMED.

NEWMAN, <u>Circuit Judge</u>, concurs in the result.

---

[5] Similarly, we reject the idea that any "property" right in the finality of a divorce decree was taken <u>by the United States</u> inasmuch as the subject divorce decrees were reopened pursuant to state action. <u>See</u>, <u>e.g.</u>, Tex. R. Ct. 329b; N.M.R. Civ. P. Sec. 1-060; Wash. Ct. R. 60(b).

APPENDIX F

Treatment of Military Retirement Pay

The following illustrate the various definitions used for military retired pay.

Uniformed Services Former Spouses' Protection Act Position

The USFSPA states, "Subject to the limitations of this section, a court may treat disposable retired or retainer pay..., either as property solely of the member or as property of the member and his spouse in accordance with the laws of the jurisdiction of such court."

Department of Defense Position on Military Retired Pay

The Department of Defense views military retired pay as reduced pay for reduced services. Military retired pay is defined in Federal statutes as income; it is treated as income in a tax court; and it is treated as income in a bankruptcy court. The distinction between the DoD position and the USFSPA on military retired pay is that state courts **may** treat it as property in a divorce action.

According to the Office of the Assistant Secretary of Defense for Military Manpower and Personnel Policy, "Military retired (and retainer) pay cannot be categorized as simply wages, pension, property, income, or any other single item. Military retired pay is a complex element of the compensation package used to help provide the quantity, quality, and mix of skilled personnel needed to meet national defense requirements. Although definition (27), Section 101, Title 10, USC states that "pay" includes retired pay and retainer pay, the complete definition of military retired pay can only be prescribed by the entire body of law that pertains to it."

Thus, military retired pay is the only form of compensation that is simultaneously treated as income and property. The treatment of military retired pay as (1) income for purposes of support and alimony (under the provisions of the state laws and under 42 U.S.C.§659 et.seq., and as (2) property under the community property and equitable distribution laws of most states, raises the question: How can it be both?

McCarty Case (U.S. Supreme Court) and I.R.S. Positions

In the *McCarty* decision, the U.S. Supreme Court said retired pay was "reduced compensation for reduced current services." The I.R.S. says it is wages and, as such, is taxable as income. The I.R.S. also treats that portion of retired pay which was divided as property and is received in the form of periodic payments by former spouses, as alimony and taxable as income. There are exceptions to this, of course, but generally the statement is true.

Comptroller General Position

The Comptroller General, in Decision B-221190 (February 11, 1986), states, ". . . the Act in no way redefines retired pay but merely allows state courts to treat this current compensation as divisible property if permissible under state law."

Military Coalition Position and The Retired Officers Association

For years these two organizations' position on military retired pay is that it is "current reduced pay for current reduced services." Their rationale is "based in part on the fact that in cases of a national defense emergency, retirees could be recalled to active duty."[1]

TROA and other associations in The Military Coalition decided to support the Kansas military retirees in their appeal to the U.S. Supreme Court in *Barker v. Kansas.* (See below.)

Debates (3 examples) in Other State Courts[2]

Michigan. In 1989, the U.S. Supreme Court ruled as discriminatory a Michigan tax scheme that permitted the taxation of federal civilian retirees' retired pay while exempting its own state retirees from similar taxes.[3] This ruling forced tax law changes in dozens of states. As a result, military retirees in other states thought they, too, would be treated (for income tax purposes) as their civilian counterparts were treated.[4] This was not to be the case.

Kansas. On July 12, 1991, the Kansas Supreme Court declared that military retired pay is reduced income for reduced services to the government. In that action, the Kansas court denied an estimated $80 million in refunds to nearly 16,000 military retirees living in the state. In other words, Kansas upheld the state income tax levied on military retired pay, but not on most federal civil servants. And, it felt that such a discriminatory action was a permissible exception to the prohibition of the federal statute. Since Kansas did not believe the military retired pay was "legally" a pension, they felt justified in claiming that it did not fall under the 1989 U.S. Supreme Court ruling (that states must tax federal, state and local government pensions at the same rate).

In their reasoning, the Kansas Justices said that "military pensions are different because their recipients have not really retired but merely have stepped down from active duty, still subject to recall."[5] This case went all the way to the U.S. Supreme Court. (See below.)

Colorado. On September 16, 1991, the Colorado Supreme Court ruled that the military retired pay is a pension. Obviously, the military retirees who picked Colorado to settle down had something to celebrate about, for the ruling put as much as $5,000 back into their pockets in refunds for income taxes collected under a discriminatory tax law repealed in 1989.

Under the old law, retired people under the age of 55 could exclude $20,000 of their annual pensions from state income taxes, but military retirees were singled out and limited to a $2,000 exclusion.

U.S. Supreme Court and Kansas

On November 27, 1991, the justices agreed to review the Kansas decision (*Barker v. Kansas*) that held that retired pay is reduced compensation for reduced service, and not a pension. On March 3, 1992, the case was argued. Then, on April 21, 1992, the Justices handed down the following decision:

States may not tax military retired pay if they exempt state and local government pensions from state income tax.

The Court held that, for purposes of preventing discrimination against military retirees, military retired pay is to be considered deferred pay for past services, like the pensions of state and local government retirees. (See Appendix D.)

APPENDIX F ENDNOTES

1. See *The Retired Officer Magazine*, November 1991, page 12+.

2. The July 5, 1993 issue of the *Air Force Times* carried a state-by-state breakdown on the U.S. Supreme Court's June 18, 1993, ruling in favor of military and civilian retirees in Virginia. The Supreme Court has ruled that Virginia illegally taxed military (and federal) retirement pay while exempting the retirement income of state retirees. The most recent update on the various cases pending in the states appears in the January 24, 1994, issue (page 20) of the *Air Force Times*.

3. The Michigan case was *Davis v. Michigan*. The new law is found at 4 U.S.C. §111.

4. The U.S. Supreme Court ruling in *Davis v. Michigan* did not specifically mention military retired pay. It was widely assumed, however, that it would fall under the general heading of federal pensions.

5. *Barker v. Kansas*, July 12, 1992. Kansas also taxes the pensions of former foreign service officers, public health officers, and members of the Central Intelligence Agency. The Kansas Supreme Court said it would take another case to determine if those taxes are valid.

APPENDIX G

Public Laws Affecting Military Divorces

The following is a non-inclusive list of the major public laws affecting former spouses. (Some of these laws had expiration dates or inclusive dates for their applicability; thus, they may not apply to prospective divorces.) The remaining section identifies applicable portions of the *Code of Federal Regulations* that apply to related actions.

PL 97-248 (1982) **The Tax Equity and Fiscal Responsibility Amendment (TEFRA) of the Social Security Act**

Enables a former spouse of an active duty service member to file for involuntary allotments to be taken from the member's monthly pay for payment of overdue spousal and/or child support without having to pursue court proceedings.

PL 97-252 (1982) **The Uniformed Services Former Spouses' Protection Act**

Authorizes state courts to treat military retired pay in the same manner they treat other pensions; authorizes the retired pay to be treated as property (vs. income). Provides for direct pay from the military finance center of a percentage of the retired pay and/or for child/spousal support when the marriage lasted 10 years or more during shared active duty time of the member. Authorizes commissary, exchange, and medical care, including CHAMPUS, for unremarried former spouses who were married for at least 20 years during active duty service, if divorced after February 1, 1983. Authorizes naming the former spouse as SBP beneficiary.

PL 98-94 (1984)

Allows military members who divorced before USFSPA to designate a former spouse as beneficiary of the SBP if member was a participant at the time of retirement.

163

PL 98-525 (1984) 1985 Defense Authorization Act

Extended military medical care and shopping privileges to 20-20-20s divorced before February 1, 1983 and medical care only to 20-20-15s divorced before February 1, 1983. Directed DoD to develop a plan for all former spouses to convert from military medical care to a private health insurance plan. Extended military care for two years or until the health plan was in place to 20-20-15s divorced after April 1, 1985. Enables the former spouse to ask for a "deemed election" of the SBP if the member does not file the application.

PL 99-145 (1985) 1986 Defense Authorization Act

Requires spousal concurrence for a member to waive SBP or select less than the maximum coverage. Creates a 2-tier system (55% until age 62, 35% after) for the SBP instead of a social security offset; benefits for those already enrolled are to be computed under the most favorable system. Creates new "former spouse" and "former spouse and child" categories with lower premiums than the former "insurable interest" category.

PL 99-661 (1986) 1987 Defense Authorization Act

Allows state courts[1] to order that a former spouse be designated as SBP beneficiary.[2] Extends medical coverage for 20-20-15s until a health plan is in place. Lowers the age at which a surviving spouse may remarry, without losing SBP benefits, from 60 to 55. Limits the deduction of Chapter 61 (DoD) (10 U.S.C. §1201 et.seq.) disability pay in determining disposable pay to be considered in the percentage awarded at the time of retirement. Eliminates the deduction for life insurance premiums in determining disposable pay. (The amendments made in this law apply to court orders issued on or after the date of the enactment of the Act.)

---

[1]Although state courts were authorized to order SBP, this did not mean that a state court would order it if the state law did not provide for such. For example, it wasn't until July 1, 1992, that Virginia passed such a bill. Before then, a court could not order the member to designate the former spouse as SBP beneficiary, even though the federal law allowed for it.

[2]Mandating SBP for the first spouse can present real problems in providing for a second spouse, particularly when the first spouse has already been awarded a share of the retired pay, and the second spouse could be the one who is married to the member longer.

PL 100-27 (1987) 1988 Defense Authorization Act

Extended medical care for certain spouses from April 1, 1988 until December 31.

PL 100-456 (1988) 1989 Defense Authorization Act

Changes the cost of the SBP to a straight 6.5% except for a few with a low base amount who are grandfathered.[3]

PL 101-189 (November 1989) 1990 Defense Authorization Act

Authorized a supplemental survivor benefit plan (changed 10 U.S.C. 1457 et.seq., added Subchapter III to Chapter 73, Part II, of Title 10). Enables participants in the SBP to provide a supplemental annuity for the spouse or former spouse beginning when the participant dies or when the spouse or former spouse becomes 62 years of age, whichever is later, in order to offset the effects of the two-tier annuity computation under the SBP.

PL 101-510 (November 1990) 1991 Defense Authorization Act

Prohibits the reopening of pre-McCarty divorce cases for the purpose of dividing military retired pay. Placed a two-year limit (until November 1992) on payments to those who did reopen pre-McCarty cases and were awarded a share of the retirement pay. Redefines disposable pay to eliminate the deduction of taxes and personal debts for those divorced after February 4, 1991.

PROCEDURAL REGULATIONS

The following citations are representative of some of the procedural regulations applicable to uniformed services retirement pay. They are listed by U.S.C. title.

Title 26--IRS

Income Tax, Applicable rules relating to certain reduced uniformed services retirement pay, 26 CFR 1.122-1

---

[3]In most cases, this was a favorable change, as it reduced the monthly premium.

Title 32--National Defense

Eligible beneficiaries and health benefits authorized, 32 CFR 728.31

Former Spouse Payments from Retired Pay, Definitions, 32 CFR 63.3

Garnishment of pay of AF members and employees only for child support or alimony obligations, 32 CFR 818.20

Title 38--Department of Veterans' Affairs

Benefits at DIC rates in certain cases when death is not service connected, 38 CFR 3.22

APPENDIX H

H.R. 2200 -- As Originally Proposed

102D CONGRESS
1ST SESSION

H.R. 2200

To amend title 10, United States Code, to revise the rules relating to the payment of retired pay of retired members of the Armed Forces to former spouses pursuant to court orders.

IN THE HOUSE OF REPRESENTATIVES
May 2, 1991
Mr. DORNAN of California introduced the following bill; which was referred to the Committee on Armed Services

---

A BILL

To amend title 10, United States Code, to revise the rules relating to the payment of retired pay of retired members of the Armed Forces to former spouses pursuant to court orders.

Be it enacted by the Senate and House of Representatives of the United States of America in Congress assembled,

SECTION 1. SHORT TITLE.
This Act may be cited as the "Uniformed Services Former Spouses Protection Act Fairness Amendments of 1991."

SEC. 2. REVISION IN THE TERMINATION PROVISION FOR PAYMENTS FROM DISPOSABLE RETIRED PAY.
(a) IN GENERAL.--Section 1408(d) of title 10, United States Code,

is amended by striking paragraph (4) and substituting the following new paragraph:

"(4)(A) Payments from the disposable retired pay of a member as a result of treating retired pay as property of the member and the former spouse pursuant to this section shall terminate in accordance with the terms of the applicable court order, but not later than the date of remarriage of the former spouse, the date of the death of the member or the date of the death of the spouse or former spouse to whom payments are being made, whichever occurs first. Payments under this section which are or have been terminated as the result of the former spouse's remarriage shall not be reinstated on account of the termination of the former spouse's subsequent marriage.

"(B) Nothing in this section shall be construed to relieve a member of liability for the payment of child support required by a court order.

"(C) The Secretary shall, within 90 days of the date of enactment of this Act, promulgate regulations establishing procedures for ascertaining the current marital status of former spouse's receiving payments of a member's retired pay under this section, and shall, with respect to former spouses who have entered into a remarriage, terminate such payments by not later than 180 days from the date of enactment of this Act".

(b) DEFINITION OF "REMARRIAGE."--Subsection (a) of such section is amended by adding the following new paragraph:

"(7) The term 'remarriage' means any marriage subsequent to the termination by court order of a marriage between a member and his or her spouse, regardless of whether the subsequent marriage is terminated by (A) a court order or (B) death of the subsequent spouse."

(c) EFFECTIVE DATE.--The amendment made by subsection (a) shall apply with respect to payments of a member's retired pay by the Secretary payable 180 days after the date of enactment of this Act.

SEC. 3. AWARD OF RETIRED PAY TO BE BASED ON RETIREE'S LENGTH OF SERVICE AND PAY GRADE AT TIME OF DIVORCE.

(a) IN GENERAL.--Section 1408(c) of title 10, United States Code, is amended by adding a new paragraph (5) as follows:

"(5)(A) In the case of a member as to whom a final decree of divorce, dissolution, annulment, or legal separation is issued before the date the member begins to receive retired pay, the disposable retired pay of the member that a court may treat in the manner described in paragraph (1) shall be computed based on the pay grade and lengths of service of the member while married that are creditable for purposes of calculating entitlements to basic pay and to retired pay on the date of the final decree. Amounts so calculated shall be increased by the cumulative percentage of increases in retired pay between the date of the final decree and the effective date of the member's retirement.

"(B) With respect to payments to former spouses from a member's disposable retired pay pursuant to court orders issued prior to the effective date of this Act, the Secretary shall, within 90 days of the effective date of this Act, recompute the amounts of those payments in accordance with paragraph (A) hereof, and, within 180 days of the effective date of this Act, adjust the amount of disposable retired pay payable to the former spouse accordingly."

(b) EFFECTIVE DATE.--The amendment made by subsection (a) shall apply with respect to court orders issued on or after June 25, 1981.

SEC. 4. EFFECTIVE DATE; PROHIBITION OF CERTAIN RETROACTIVE COURT ORDERS.

(a) IN GENERAL.--Subsection (e) of section 555 of Public Law 101-510 is amended by striking out "two-year" and inserting in lieu thereof "one-year."

SEC. 5. LIMITATION ON TIME FOR SEEKING DIVISION OF RETIRED PAY. (a) IN GENERAL.--Subsection (c)(4) of section 1408 of title 10, United States Code, is amended to read as follows:

"(4) A court may not treat the disposable retired pay of a member in the manner described in paragraph (1) unless--

"(A) the court has jurisdiction over the member by reason of (A) his residence, other than because of military assignment, in the territorial jurisdiction of the court, (B) his domicile in the territorial jurisdiction of the court, or (C) his consent to the jurisdiction of the court. However, if the court, in the final decree, does not treat or reserve jurisdiction to treat the disposable retired pay of the member in the manner described in paragraph (1), then in any subsequent judicial proceeding to treat the disposable retired pay of the member in the manner described in paragraph (1), the jurisdiction of the court must be separately established at the time the subsequent judicial proceeding is initiated, based on the criteria in this subparagraph (A);

"(B) the member's spouse or former spouse makes proper application to a court for division or partition of retired pay of the member as property of the member and the member's spouse or former spouse within two years of the date of a final decree of divorce, dissolution, annulment, or legal separation, including a court ordered, ratified, or approved property settlement incident to such a decree."

(b) EFFECTIVE DATE.--The amendment made by subsection (a) shall apply with respect to final decrees issued after the date of the enactment of this Act.

SEC. 6.TREATMENT OF DISABILITY PAY UNDER CHAPTER 61.
(a) IN GENERAL.--Subsection (a)(4)(E) of section 1408 of title 10, United States Code, is amended to read as follows:
"(E) in the case of a member entitled to retired pay under chapter 61 of this title, are equal to the amount of retired pay of the member under that chapter computed using the percentage of the member's disability on the date when the member was retired (or the date on which the member's name was placed on the temporary disability retired list), and no court shall include amounts of disability pay so calculated as property of the member and the member's spouse or former spouse subject to division under this section."

(b) EFFECTIVE DATE.--The amendment made by subsection (a) shall apply with respect to court orders issued on, before or after the date of enactment of this Act.

SEC. 7.PROHIBITION ON DISTRIBUTIONS OF ACTIVE DUTY PAY.
(a) IN GENERAL.--Section 1408 of the title 10, United State Code, is amended—

(1) by striking in its entirety subparagraph (c)(3) and
(2) by adding a new subparagraph (c)(3) to read as follows:

"(3) No court may, pursuant to this section, order a member to apply for retirement or retire at a particular time in order to effectuate any payment under this section, nor may any court order a member to make any payment pursuant to this section out of the member's active duty income earned on or after the date the member first becomes eligible for retirement, nor may any court order a member to make any pre-retirement payment equivalent to a payment which would otherwise be made pursuant to this section had the member retired and commenced receiving retired pay. A payment shall be deemed to be a pre-retirement payment prohibited by this subparagraph if the payment (i) is ordered by a court to be made by a member on active duty commencing on the date a member first becomes eligible to retire from military service and prior to actual retirement (ii) equals or approximates, in amount or percentage, the amount or percentage which would be paid to a former spouse had the member retired on or about the date the court orders payments to begin. Any retired member recalled to active duty after initial retirement shall not be ordered by any court to commence or continue payments to a former spouse resulting from the treatment of retired pay as property, while the member is on active duty."

(3) by adding at the end of subsection (d) the following new paragraph:

"(6) In no event shall the Secretary make any payment under this section from a member's active duty pay."

(b) EFFECTIVE DATE.—The amendments made by subsection (a) shall apply to any payment prohibited by subsection (a) and due to be paid on or after the date of enactment of this Act pursuant to a court order.

APPENDIX I

Survivor Benefit Plan (SBP)

The full text for the SBP can be found in Title 10 of the U.S. Code. The following is a summary of changes to that law.

Approved Pub.L. 92-425 (1972). Amendments: Pub.L. 93-406 (1974) granted special tax treatment for SBP. Pub.L. 94-496 (1976) mandated certain deductions from retired pay. Pub.L. 95-397 (1978) eliminated the Social Security offset for a working widow not eligible to receive Social Security benefits because of her income from employment. A Reserve Component SBP was established. Pub.L. 96-402 (1980), among other changes, modified the Social Security offset; suspended voluntary SBP participation from certain disabled retirees. Pub.L. 97-35 (1981) authorized a one-year open enrollment period. Pub.L. 97-252 (1982) (and subsequent amendments to USFSPA) provided for former spouse coverage. Pub.L. 98-525 (1984) changed the Social Security offset rules, as did Pub.L. 99-145 (1985), which established a two-tier system relative to the Social Security offset. Pub.L. 99-145 also required spousal consent before the member can decline SBP or elect less than maximum coverage or coverage for a child only. Pub.L. 99-576 (1986) permits the deduction of SBP costs from VA disability compensation. Pub.L. 99-661 (1987), among other changes, authorized state courts to order members to participate in SBP. Pub.L. 100-224 (1987) allows for a concurrent increase in SBP base amount whenever military retired pay is increased. Pub.L. 100-456 (1988) makes changes relative to surviving spouses of members who died before November 1, 1953. Pub.L. 101-189 (National Defense Authorization Act for FY 1990) (1989) provides a revised premium computation for SBP annuities, to 6.5 percent of the amount selected. Those who became members of the uniformed services before March 1, 1990, are grandfathered, and have the option of whichever formula is more advantageous to them (provides the lowest cost).

APPENDIX J

Military Coalition

Involvement on the Hill is Assumed and Necessary

Involvement of military organizations in defense legislation and national affairs is an accepted activity on the "Hill." The late Rep. Bill Nichols (D-AL), former Chairman of the House Armed Services Subcommittee on Military Personnel and Compensation, said of the Council's involvement: "We are faced with a wide variety of issues, and it is very difficult for members of Congress to have detailed knowledge of all of them. Letters from military personnel and retirees assist in acquiring this knowledge. I think you serve as an important intermediary between your membership and the Congress. You take the expressed feelings of your members and focus those views on the legislation before the Congress."

Representing a combined membership of 3.5 million active, reserve, and retired military members and their families is an organization known as the Military Coalition. Its member organizations (between 23-25) are united in their efforts to provide a strong voice in Congress and within the Department of Defense and the Department of Veterans Affairs. The group was formed in 1986 in response to the Gramm-Rudman-Hollings bill to cancel the cost-of-living-adjustments (COLAs) for military and federal civilian retirees. The Coalition's mission was then, as it is now, a "quest for equity," be it the issue of COLAs or retired pay and USFSPA.

Leadership

Leadership of the Military Coalition is chaired jointly by two military retirees. Colonel Paul W. Arcari, USAF-Ret., is director of Government Relations for The Retired Officers Association (TROA). Sergeant Major Michael Ouellette, is the legislative counsel for the Non Commissioned Officers Association (NCOA). Both have extensive experience on "the Hill."

175

How the Coalition Derives Its Agenda

Each organization in the Military Coalition has its own agenda, and the issue of divorce and military retired pay may not be high on that agenda. While professing to administer to the needs of the members, many of the Coalition member organizations have not addressed the USFSPA issue in any depth. Unless the issue is brought up at the lowest level in an individual organization, i.e., local chapter, it is unlikely it will proceed to the national level where the national headquarters can take a position based upon a resolution. The USFSPA is considered too much of a "hot" issue, and one not affecting too many people (a point that could be disputed). Many organization leaders feel the issue is too narrow for their members, and feel that broader issues, i.e., affecting the majority, are more appropriate.

Nonetheless, anyone planning to join any of the member organizations or who is already a member, might do well to seek out the organization's position on USFSPA. Lack of equity legislation has been blamed on the fact that people just don't know about USFSPA. Any reader of this book is encouraged to write the authors if your association with an organization has yielded positive action on the USFSPA issue.

The Coalition arrives at its agenda via a "rule of three." If three or more of its member associations object to a proposed initiative, the initiative does not get placed on the Coalition's legislative agenda. All is not lost, however, with a particular issue, as smaller subgroups within the Coalition may still put forth a lobbying effort. The National Military Family Association, a member of the coalition, has generally been opposed to the other members' position on equity changes to the USFSPA.

Member Organizations

Air Force Association	National Guard Association of the U.S.
Air Force Sergeants Association	National Military Family Association
Association of Military Surgeons	Naval Enlisted Reserve Association
Association of the U.S. Army	Naval Reserve Association
Commissioned Officers of the PHS	Navy League of the U.S.
CWO & WO Association, USCG	Non Commissioned Officers Association
Enlisted Association of the NGUS	Reserve Officers Association
Fleet Reserve Association	The Military Chaplains Association
Jewish War Veterans	The Retired Enlisted Association
Marine Corps League	The Retired Officers Association
Marine Corps ROA	U.S. Army Warrant Officers Association
National Association for	USCG Chief Petty Officer Association
Uniformed Services/Society	United Armed Forces Association
of Military Widows	

APPENDIX K

Contacting Your Elected Representatives

Why Your Input Is Needed

If you think that you are caught totally by surprise by some laws or complain that you just "didn't hear about it," then put yourself in the shoes of your elected officials, and consider that they, too, are uninformed and misinformed, even by their staff, on a lot that is happening. Impossible, you say? Consider that in an average year, the *Federal Register* alone turns out some **63,000 pages** (9-foot high stack) on rules and procedures affecting all aspects of our lives.

It is impossible for your elected representatives to know everything that is going on—but, at the same time, it is possible for them to know something that is going on. And they learn it from their constituents—you. Our government needs the active participation of those who are directly affected by any proposed government legislation. Indeed, our legislators, their staff, and civil servants count on help from interested parties to resolve the issues that result in legislative compromises.

Before You Write or Visit

Just as you do when preparing for a job interview, you should gather as much information as possible about your senator's or representative's background. The information you acquire could be mentioned in your letter or during your visit. This includes their hometown, committee assignments, specific interests and background of those interests.

Once you have this information or find you have something in common (you admire their position on a particular issue), then say so in your letter or during your visit.

Writing a Member of Congress

Senators and representatives do pay attention to their mail—they know what it takes to get reelected! While they do receive form letters, they are not nearly as effective as personal letters, where the constituent provides some personal information as to how or why a particular issue affects them. It goes without saying that the letter *must* be short, informed, and polite.

Here are some pointers that will help you make points with your congressmen and women:

1. Keep your letter to one typewritten page, two pages at the most. Never write on the back of a page. If you cannot type the letter, then write neatly in longhand, or better yet, print.

2. First paragraph—state your purpose and stick with only one subject or issue. The succeeding paragraphs must support your main topic.

3. If you are writing in response to a bill, cite it by name and number. If you do not know it, call Capitol Hill to find it out. The U.S. Capitol switchboard can be reached at (202) 224-3121.

4. Personalize your letter—cite facts and support your position about how the (proposed) legislation (will) affect you and others. Avoid emotional arguments or threats to withhold your vote in the next election.

5. If you have strong beliefs about the legislation and believe your official should oppose it, then state so, indicating the adverse effects it is likely to have. If you have a solution, propose it!

6. Ask your representative where he or she stands on the proposed legislation, but do not demand their support. Do not be surprised, however, when you receive a response that is neutral. Senators and Representatives must take into consideration the views of their entire constituency; perhaps your position will be heard the next time the issue is addressed.

7. Don't forget to provide your name and return address.

The address to write is:

The Honorable_____   The Honorable_____
U. S. Senate   U.S. House of Representatives
Washington DC 20510   Washington DC 20515

Dear Senator_____Dear Representative_____

Meeting a Member of Congress

Visiting your elected officials is a very effective way to take the letter-writing initiative one step further. A visit emphasizes your interest in a bill and reinforces your beliefs in the legislative process. Visiting, however, requires you to adhere to a particular set of courtesies.

1. Make an appointment--state your subject, the amount of time you will need, and anyone else who will be attending with you.

2. If a group is going, it is imperative that you select one person to be the spokesperson and that you all agree on what will be said. The representative will, in all likelihood, ask questions of individuals.

3. It is imperative that you **know the facts**. In this case, you must know the bill title and number, and its legislative content.

4. Your spokesperson must present the facts in a concise, organized, and positive manner.

5. Relate both the positive and negative impacts of the legislation, the problems it corrects and the problems it poses, along with a different approach, if possible.

6. Leave fact sheets or an information packet with your elected officials. Encourage the official and his or her staff to ask questions.

7. Your final requests when leaving are: ask for favorable consideration, thank the congressman/woman for their time and courtesy, and leave promptly.

Software to Help You Contact Congress

If you think that writing your representatives (including senators) in Congress is too much trouble, then you might be interested in a software package from Contact Software International, Inc., that takes all the work out of doing so (in other words—no more excuses for **not** writing Congress on this or any other matter!). The software, "Write Your Congressman!" (IBM/compatible; requires DOS 3.1 or higher, a hard drive and 640k RAM available; under $50) gives you several format choices: personalized letters, form letters, envelopes and mailing labels.

Since it provides the correct format for salutations and closings, all you need do is type in whatever you want to say—opinions, complaints, and suggestions. If you are in a really big hurry to get the attention of your congressperson's ear, the software will produce a fax cover sheet for you and even dial the congressional office for delivering your "2 cents' worth" via your modem, as it includes fax numbers for all of them.

If your excuse is you don't know the name of your congressperson, then you will have to find another excuse. This software not only will produce the name, it will ensure that your form of address is the correct for etiquette purposes. So, having to wonder whether your salutation is the right one is something you won't have to worry about ever again. Finally, the software will keep a log of your correspondence with individual members of Congress.

One last note here--once you purchase the software, you can buy a special membership in the nonpartisan legislative research organization that inspired the product, the National Write Your Congressman, Inc. (NWYC). You will receive monthly updates on major legislation in Congress, plus the voting records of each representative and senator.

APPENDIX L

Checklist for Interviewing an Attorney

TYPE	QUESTIONS TO ASK AND ASSESS	+-
EXPERIENCE WITH MILITARY DIVORCES	1. How long has the attorney been handling military divorce cases? 2. What is his/her knowledge of the jurisdiction requirements for military personnel (if you are active duty)? 3. Jurisdiction: a. If yours is an out-of-state case (e.g., the spouse has had you served from another state), what is the attorney's experience in working with out-of-state attorneys? b. The attorney's knowledge about the law in the other state (such that she can advise you on whether to initiate a divorce suit in your current state or accept jurisdiction in the other state) 4. What is the local court's track record regarding military retired pay division? 5. How have the local courts treated the division of military retired pay for non-working spouses? 6. What is the attorney's personal beliefs toward military spouses? 7. How many cases has the attorney handled with the military member as the plaintiff? With the spouse as the plaintiff? 8. What do they know about the USFSPA? SBP? Other insurance alternatives?	

TYPE	QUESTIONS TO ASK AND ASSESS	+-

FEES	1. Does the attorney require a written agreement before being retained?
	
	2. Regarding the attorney's retainer:
	  a. How much is it?
	  b. Is any of it refunded if the divorce turns out to be processed quickly and without problems?
	  c. What is the hourly fee?
	  d. If the attorney has to appear in court for you, what are the rates? Is it an hourly fee or a flat rate?
	
	3. Regarding the bill:
	  a. Are you billed monthly?
	  b. Is the entire amount required to be paid each month?
	  c. Can you work out a payment schedule?
	  d. What detail is included on the bills?
	  e. Does the lawyer's fee include expenses (some do) or are expenses itemized separately?
	  f. Are phone calls billed at a minimum of a certain time (e.g., 15 minutes)?
	
	4. Does the attorney have a paralegal do any of the work? If so, are you charged less for the paralegal's services? (Some attorneys' fees are inclusive--their hourly rate covers the secretary and other staff.)	

GENERAL WORKING RELATIONSHIP	1. If necessary, will the attorney call you at your home instead of at work? 2. Will the attorney provide you (if you want) with drafts of all motions before they are signed and sent to the opposing attorney or court? 3. What is the attorney's opinion as to the difficulty of your case and what it might involve?	

TYPE	QUESTIONS TO ASK AND ASSESS	+-
YOUR SPECIFIC QUESTIONS	1.	
	2.	
	3.	
	4.	
	5.	
	6.	
	7.	
	8.	
	9.	
	10.	

Your suggestions or recommendations to improve this checklist are welcome. Is there any particular aspect about your attorney or the way your case was handled that could benefit others? If so, we would like to hear from you.

Please send your comments to ARA (Attn: Book Authors), 7564 Trade St., San Diego, CA 92121-2412.

APPENDIX M

Preparing For Your Attorney:
What You Both Need to Know

TYPE	INFORMATION YOU NEED TO OBTAIN AND COMPILE	√
BASIC INFORMATION	1. Date & place of marriage 2. Prior marriage (& divorce) date 3. Birthdates/Ages of husband (H) & wife (W) 4. Children & their ages 5. Educational level of H & W 6. General health of H & W 7. General work experience of H & W 8. Total yearly income (last 3 years) for both 9. Unusual contributions (monetary & nonmonetary) of both during the marriage 10. Standard of living established 11. Financial needs and resources of H & W 12. Any agreements between the H & W 13. Circumstances contributing to the divorce 14. Military pay grade and years of service 15. Estimated military retirement income	

MILITARY SUMMARY	1. Listing of all your military assignments
	    -when, where, how long
	    -accompanied or unaccompanied
	2. Indicate whether your spouse worked (and the approximately yearly income) for each assignment period
	3. Anticipating or already receiving VA disability compensation?
	4. Status of spouse (eligible for future military medical care, and commissary and exchange privileges?)	

TYPE	INFORMATION YOU NEED TO OBTAIN AND COMPILE	√

PERSONAL & REAL PROPERTY	Inventory all your assets--marital and non marital
	
	    automobiles
	
	    furniture
	
	    houses
	
	    land	

FINANCIAL STATUS For each account, provide the following: - date opened - beginning balance - current balance - average & frequency of deposits - yearly deposits	1. Complete an Income and Expense sheet (monthly budget). 2. Active Duty—a copy of your Leave and Earnings Statement 3. Retiree—a copy of your monthly retiree's account statement 4. Reservist—a copy of your weekend drill statements and the most recent point accounting statement. 5. Copy of the last three years income tax returns. 6. Other financial assets—e.g., savings accounts, credit unions, savings bonds. 7. Retirement plans (IRAs, 401k, TSP--if civil service, employer plan). 8. Outstanding debts (e.g., car loan, school loans, mortgage, credit cards). 9. Insurance policies (term, whole life and cash value, disability, property, supplemental health, etc.) 10. Estimate (both husband and wife) future income (e.g., selling a second home). 11. Estimate (both husband and wife) future expenses (e.g., college for the children, returning to school) 12. Statement on spouse's ability to afford an attorney.	

APPENDIX N

Resources

This section is a list (by no means, inclusive) of some sources of information that you may wish to consult or read for further information. While some of the resources do not address purely legal issues related to the USFSPA or military retirement, many contain information that is useful in establishing the positions of the parties in a divorce and sorting out the facts. This section is grouped according to the type of resource that is available, with a short commentary, in some instances. Some legal references are included for those who are interested in legal research or reading the original law.

Every attempt has been made to include valid addresses and telephone numbers. However, given their changing nature, we apologize for any errors you may find. (Let us know the correct data.) Resources are listed in alphabetical order by subject and alphabetically by topic within the main subject.

1. <u>AMERICAN BAR ASSOCIATION</u>

750 North Lakeshore Drive Chicago, IL 60611
Tel.: (312) 988-5000.

Within the ABA, Family Law Section, Federal Legislation and Procedures Committee, is the Federal and Military Pension Legislation Subcommittee. The chair is Marshal S. Willick, Esq., 330 South Third St., #960, Las Vegas NV 89101. Tel: (702) 384-3440. (Note: This subcommittee was very pro-spouse regarding equity changes proposed in 1990.)

There is also the Standing Committee on Legal Assistance for Military Personnel. The chairperson (as of January 1994) is Marilyn Barmash [Tel: 312-988-5618)]. The contact for military law at the ABA is Marilyn Neforas [Tel: (312) 988-5596]. Neither of these two chairpersons is ex-military.

2. ASSOCIATIONS

Pro-military member on the USFSPA:

American Retirees Association   Washington Operations Office
7564 Trade Street   2009 N. 14th St Suite 300
San Diego CA 92121-2412   Arlington VA 22201-2514
Tel: (619) 239-9000   Tel: (703) 527-3065

Pro-spouse on the USFSPA:

EX-POSE (Ex-Partners of Servicemen (Women) for Equality)
PO Box 11191 Alexandria VA 22312   Tel: (703) 941-5844

Founded in 1980, active membership numbers around 3500.
This organization serves the interests of the military spouse by
educating them on their benefits after divorce. They publish a
bimonthly newsletter and a booklet entitled "A Guide to Military
Wives Facing Separation or Divorce."

Pro-Men

Men's Rights Association (aka Men's Defense Association)
17854 Lyons Forest Lake MN 55025-8854
Tel: (612) 464-7887   Fax: (612) 464-7135

Founded in 1971, MRA has approximately 6000 members.
Their monthly newsletter (approximately 28 pages), The Lib-
erator, is full of issues related to divorce, particularly child support. A quarterly column entitled, "Soldiers, Sailors, Airmen,"
addresses military issues (including divorce). They also publish a number of very inexpensive reference materials and a
small divorce handbook, and are a major source for information on men and child custody problems. Some of the titles
available and their prices are: "Divorce: What All Should Know,"
$6; "Educate-a-Judge package," $7; "Alimony/support defenses,
$5; Child Custody Preparation, $3; Sex Abuse Charges in Divorce. $5; Child Abuse Allegations: Discovery Pointers, $5;
Preparing Witnesses, $5; Medical Exam Falsehoods, $10; Bib-
liography and List of Experts, $1. Membership in MRA is $20.
Annual subscription rates for the monthly newsletter are $24.
MRA also has a network of lawyers who charge reasonable
fees, as well as a list of computer bulletin boards for legal issues related to men, divorce, and child custody cases. (If you
do write MRA, please mention you learned about them through
this book.)

Other Associations

Alliance of Retired Military (A.R.M)—4174 South Parker Road, Suite 202, Aurora CO 80014. Carl F. Gail, Executive Director. This organization is active in Colorado, and is an offshoot of an A.R.A. chapter.

Military Retiree Spouses (M.R.S.), now formally disbanded, was established in 1986 as a companion organization to A.R.A. for the military retiree spouses. With the passage of changes to eliminate the retroactivity feature of FSPA, and the legal matters of its founders, a decision was made to disband.

Retired Military Nurse Corps Association (RMNCA)—P.O. Box 39235 Seana Station, San Antonio TX 78218. The RMNCA is pro-USFSPA reform and has considerable political clout.

3. BOOKS

Friedman, James T. *The Divorce Handbook—Your Basic Guide to Divorce.* NY: Random House, 1984.

This book is packed full of things—checklists, guides, sample schedules and worksheets for things such as assets and liabilities, child support schedules, initial interview sheet (what the lawyer will need from you), trial outline. It is presented in a question-and-answer format, and covers the topics of choosing a lawyer, the lawyer's fees, you and your lawyer, discovery procedures, negotiation strategies, preparing for trial, child custody and support, financial hide-and-seek with your spouse, and much, much more. An excellent book to read *before* you pay your first visit to a lawyer.

HALT, *Divorce.* Washington, DC: HALT, 1319 F. St. NW #300 Washington DC 20004. See the next listing for information on HALT.

HALT, *Using A Lawyer...And What To Do If Things Go Wrong.* Washington, DC: HALT, 1985. (HALT is An Organization of Americans for Legal Reform.)

By reading this book *before* you hire an attorney, you could very well avoid having anything go wrong (not agreeing with the law doesn't count). Besides telling you how to select an attorney and what to look for, it gives excellent coverage to the kind of problems that can develop (e.g., overcharging, overlawyering) and what you can do if you feel your lawyer is ignoring you. If you are having problems with your attorney, this book can help you decide whether to fire him or her. HALT is located at 1319 F Street NW, Suite 300, Washington DC 20004. Telephone: (202) 347-9600. This particular book is under $10.

Krantzler, Melvin. *Creative Divorce.* New York: M. Evans and Co., Inc., 1974.

Although this book was published nearly 20 years ago, the information in it is still very relevant. For those who are having problems sorting out all the various dimensions of the divorce process, particularly the emotional aspects, this book can be of great help. The book is available in many public libraries and can still be purchased at bookstores.

Krantzler, Melvin. *Learning to Love Again.* New York: Thomas Y. Crowell Co., 1977.

This is a companion book to the one mentioned above. For those who do not want to repeat the problems or mistakes in their previous marriage, this book can assist by identifying the differences and actions that may have taken place in your prior marriage and help you to understand them as differences, not problems to be ignored. This book is also available on audio cassette in libraries.

Moss, Ann C. *Your Pension Rights at Divorce—What Women Need to Know.* Washington, DC: Pension Rights Center, 1991.

Although this book is geared toward women, the plans identified (including military retired pay) are applicable to either spouse. Civil Service retirement plans are also covered.

O'Connell, Marjorie A. and Kittrell, Steven D. *Federal Retirement Plans: Division of Benefits and Divorce.* Washington, DC: Divorce Taxation Education, Inc., 1987.

The section on military retirement pensions has been confused with what is enforceable through the federal government. The rest of the book is comprehensive, and it is understood that the publisher plans to correct the inadequacies regarding the section of the military retirement program.

Paul, Jordon and Margaret. *Do I Have to Give Up Me to be Loved by You?* Mpls, MN: Compcare, 1985.

This is an excellent book that everyone should read—especially if you feel that a divorce is the only solution to whatever is bothering you. This book goes through the many struggles between couples and what is really going on behind the struggles. There are four patterns to the way people communicate, and the explanations in this book are in very easy-to-understand layperson's terms. A common feeling behind many actions is fear—fear of some loss. This book explains those feelings in a way that can help couples who do not wish to go to a professional therapist or cannot afford to do so.

Schilling, Edwin III, and Wilson, Carol Ann. *Survival Manual for Women in Divorce.* Boulder, CO: Quantum Press, 1991.

Schilling, Edwin III, and Wilson, Carol Ann. *Survival Manual for Men in Divorce.* Boulder, CO: Quantum Press, 1992.

These two books are written in an easy-to-follow question-and-answer format. While not specifically geared toward military divorces, the information is, nonetheless, pertinent. Indeed, the reader of either book could probably save some money on legal fees by reviewing these books and understanding the responses and the limitations placed on both parties and the lawyer in a divorce.

Sheehy, Gail. *Passages: Predictable Crises of Adult Life.* NY: E.P. Dutton, 1974.

A classic still, you will see yourself at every stage in our lives—our twenties, thirties, forties, etc., and the major events that occur during those periods. Life is full of ups and downs and many difficulties. Unfortunately, many people think that relationships should be perfect—no conflicts (or, at least, none where *she* may disagree with *him* and vice versa!). This book is readily available in bookstores and in libraries.

Tomes, Jonathan P., Lieutenant Colonel, US Army, Retired. *The Servicemember's Legal Guide.* 2nd edition. Harrisburg, PA: Stackpole Books, 1992. ($14.95. The book is available in most military exchanges.)

This book is the only comprehensive one on just about every legal matter that a military member (and family) could be faced with. (The Reserves are also covered.) It contains chapters on divorce and separation, family members, and marriage (including overseas marriages). It is a good one to have on your reference shelf. LTC Tomes currently lives in Chicago, where he is teaching law.

Trafford, Abigail. *Crazy Time.*

This book, written in 1974 and updated, is fast becoming a standard on the divorce reading recommendation lists. It is a near diary of the start to finish process known as the "emotional" divorce, which then moves into the "legal" divorce. Readers will see that their situation is not unusual—everyone becomes a little "crazy" during this time, and the emotions that you are experiencing are the same ones divorcing couples have been experiencing for a long time. If this book does anything, it puts you in good company to know that you are NOT going crazy (at least permanently!), and that you will recover.

Uniformed Services Almanac, Inc. publishes the following annual books: *Retired Military Almanac, Reserve Forces Almanac, National Guard Almanac, Uniformed Services Almanac* (for active duty personnel).

These annual publications cost $6.95 and are available in most military exchanges or from the publisher: Uniformed Services Almanac, Inc. P.O. Box 4144, Falls Church, VA 22044. Telephone: (703) 532-1631. These books are loaded with detailed information on just about every subject imaginable that affects the military. The one for retirees includes information on the US-FSPA, SBP, state-by-state income tax information for retired military, and CHAMPUS and other retirement benefits. Both the military member and spouse would do well to review the benefits in developing an asset/liability/income/expense accounting.

4. CHAMPUS

For assistance with CHAMPUS, consult the Health Benefits Advisor at your nearest military treatment facility. The Civilian Health and Medical Program of the Uniformed Services is managed out of Aurora, CO 80045-6900, Telephone: (303) 361-3707. For an explanation of CHAMPUS benefits, see the listing of where to find information under the Uniformed Services Almanac, Inc., in section 3 of this appendix.

5. CONGRESSIONAL RESEARCH SERVICE

These reports are available only through your elected representatives.

Report 88-215A, July 1988. *Treatment of Former Spouses Under Various Federal Retirement Systems.* By Marie Morris. No special situations such as disability are discussed.

Report 89-187F, March 20, 1989. *Military Benefits for Former Spouses: Legislation and Policy Issues.* This report was updated in CRS Report No. 92-557 F, dated July 13, 1992 (same title).

6. COURT DECISIONS — Federal

Comptroller General No. B-228790.2, 3/1/91. This ruling protects former spouses from owing a sudden debt to the government when the service member is awarded a retroactive increase in disability compensation.

Eatinger v. Commissioner of Internal Revenue, U.S. Tax Court Dkt. No. 16564-89. (1990) Military retirement benefits are included as gross income to the recipient spouse as well as the military member. The retirement income was characterized as deferred compensation to the military member and not a transfer of community property to the spouse. (*Tax treatment of military retirement benefits in a divorce*)

Fern v. U.S., C.A.F.C., No. 89-1106, July 16, 1990; 908 F.2d 955 (1990 U.S. App.), 12 E.B.C. 1936. 15 Cl. Ct. 580 (1988). (*The "Unjust Taking" case*)

Mansell v. Mansell (Forbes), 109 S. Ct. 2023 (1989), 104 L.Ed.2d 675 (1989), 57 U.S.L.W. 4567, 10 E.B.C. 2521. On remand *In re Marriage of Mansell* (1989, 5th Dist) 216 Cal.App.3d 937, 265 Cal.Rptr.227, 1989 Cal.App; 217 Cal.App.3d 319, 1989 Cal.App. (Prior history: 487 U.S. 1217, 101 L.Ed.2d 904, 108 S.Ct. 2868). (*VA Disability pay waived in lieu of retired pay is not a divisible marital asset*)

McCarty v. McCarty, 453 U.S. 210 (1981), 69 L.Ed.2d 589, 101 S. Ct. 2728, 49 U.S.L.W. 4850 (1981). (*Division of military retired pay as a marital asset*)

7. COURT DECISIONS — State (listed by issue)

Civil Service Retirement (as a deduction from gross military retirement pay)

Gallegos v. Gallegos, 788 S.W.2d, 158 (1990). This appears to be the first case in Texas where the civil service salary paid to a military retiree at the time of the divorce must be deducted from the gross military retirement pay in order to determine what is "disposable" pay. (This case also affirms that VA disability retirement is excluded from division.)

Computation of Military Retirement Benefits

Kniss v. Kniss, C.A. (2d App. Dist. Calif.), Case No. 2d Civil No. B040717, July 3, 1990: This is an unpublished case that can be entered as evidence in California cases for basing the award of retired pay on the grade and service time at the time of separation (or divorce) and not at the time of retirement. (When it is based on the time of retirement, the former spouse gets a "windfall" amount that should be the sole property of the retiree.) Kniss cited two Texas cases which ruled the same way.

Berry v. Berry, 647 S.W. 2d 945 (Tex. 1983), on valuation and apportionment (at time of divorce).

Busby v. Busby, 457 S.W.2d 551 (Tex. 1970) and *Cearley v. Cearley,* 544 S.W.2d 661 (Tex. 1976) state the formula for division of military retirement benefits between spouses as: months married/months in service X final benefit X 1/2. This formula allows for the division of future military retirement benefits.

Taggart v. Taggart, 552 S.W.2 422 (Tex. 1977). Pre-McCarty formula for apportioning community property interest in retirement benefits.

Direct Payment vs. Allotment

In re marriage of Wood, 767 P.2d 338 (Or. Ct. App. 1984). Distinguishes between court orders that provide for a specific amount or percentage of disposable retirement pay and court orders that merely give offsetting judgment awards.

Disability

Berry v. Berry, 7876 S.W.2d 672 (Tex. 1990). Retroactivity of the Mansell decision.

Busby v. Busby, 457 S.W.2d 551 (Tex. 1970). Disability compensation was community property prior to the McCarty decision.

Conroy v. Conroy, 706 S.W.2d 745 Tex. App. 8th Dist. 1986).

Disability retirement pay is community property.

Miller v. Miller, 632 P.2d 732 (1981), 96 N.M. 497. The couple was divorced in NM, but stipulated the Texas law determined whether the disability compensation received by the husband could be characterized as community property. The Court ruled that the VA compensation was not subject to division, but that a trial court could award alimony where the sole source of funds for payments were disability benefits from the VA and Social Security.

Retroactivity

A New Mexico state court (2d Judicial District, Bernalillo County) decision on June 29, 1993 has ignored the 1990 amendment to USFSPA (to prohibit state courts from dividing retired pay for divorces occurring prior to June 25, 1981 and where the court did not treat the retired pay as joint property or reserve jurisdiction to do so—the retroactivity feature). The case (on appeal as of January 1994) involves retired Air Force Master Sergeant Lambert J. Gonzales of Albuquerque, in which he petitioned the NM courts to terminate USFSPA payments on the basis of the 1990 congressional amendment. The court reasoned that, under NM law, there is a "limited reservation of jurisdiction" that is incorporated into every divorce decree issued in New Mexico. Under this rationale, the conditions of the congressional amendment did not apply—and can never apply—in New Mexico. The facts of Sergeant Gonzales's case render it exactly the kind of situation Congress was trying to prevent by passing the amendment.

Unemployment Benefits (reduced) and Military Retirement

Kan v. Commonwealth of Pennsylvania, 530 A.2d 1023, 109 Pa. Commw. 184 (1987). The Unemployment Compensation Board of Review affirmed a referee's order reducing unemployment benefits by the entire amount of military retirement benefits. On appeal, the case was reversed and remanded for recalculation to deduct the amount going to the former spouse.

8. GOVERNMENT AGENCIES

Defense Finance and Accounting Service (DFAS). Commonly known as the finance center, each has attorneys on staff who are experts on USFSPA and SBP. Unlike the general toll-free telephone number that the centers have, however, most of these attorneys are not available via an 800 number. By 1995 the individual service finance centers are to have merged under a new structure, with the Denver location to handle all USFSPA issues; and the finance center in Indianapolis to handle the SBP issues.

Military Family Clearinghouse. 4015 Wilson Blvd, Suite 903, Arlington VA 22203-5190. Tel: (703) 696-4555.

This office will assist military personnel (and their families) with literature searches on various topics, including divorce. You have to read the abstracts, however, of the bibliographies, to determine whether USFSPA is addressed.

U.S. General Accounting Office—Report to the Chairman, Subcommittee on Military Personnel and Compensation, Committee on Armed Services, House of Representatives: Implementation of the Uniformed Services Former Spouses' Protection Act, GAO/NSIAD-85-4, October 24, 1984.

This report, in response to Rep. Les Aspin's 4/19/83 request (he was Chairman of the Subcommittee on Military Personnel and Compensation at the time) is a summary of the evaluation of how the Department of Defense and the military services were implementing PL 97-252. The report, besides describing the problems the services were having with implementing the law, provides some excellent examples of the tax withholding implications. If your divorce is a pre-February 1991 divorce, you might find this report interesting reading.

Department of Veterans Affairs (VA)

If a veteran or his dependents need information on what benefits they are entitled to, you now only have to make one phone call (1-800-827-1000 in the US, Puerto Rico, Virgin Islands). You will be connected with the nearest VA regional office during normal office hours. Regional offices process applications for veterans benefits and provide information and referral to those interested in VA medical care.

9. JUDGE ADVOCATE GENERAL

Every military installation will have a legal office with one or more "JAGs" and a (senior) Staff Judge Advocate. Although the military attorneys can provide some help with personal legal matters (e.g., you can get a will prepared free of charge, they will review a lease for you, etc.), the military member and the spouse are responsible for seeking a civilian attorney in divorce matters. The military attorneys can advise the military spouse of her rights and benefits, provide checklists and forms for accomplishing a separation agreement, and can assist in helping the spouse obtain family support. This assistance will only be done in person and not over the phone. The legal offices will often have literature available pertinent to the state where you are serving in.

All services require the members to support their dependents. But each individual service has its own interpretation of the Department of Defense policy on the subject. For example, the Air Force Regulation is AFR 35-18. An illustration might be where the military member has moved out of the family house and has stopped providing money to pay the rent or mortgage. Receiving housing allowance at the "with dependents" rate while refusing to support those dependents could result in a number of actions, including court-martial, nonjudicial punishment, or administrative action. In the area of child support, however, the spouse will have to produce a court-ordered document in order to have wages garnished. The local military legal office can help the spouse in terms of providing an address on where to write to submit the order. A spouse who is no longer a military dependent is not entitled to the services of the military legal office.

10. LEGAL RESEARCH SOURCES

ADMINISTRATIVE REGULATIONS

Each of the services usually has its own set of administrative regulations that cover various subjects related to SBP and USFSPA.

ENCYCLOPEDIC

Corpus Juris Secundum

6 C.J.S. *Armed Services* §§114, 116, 121, 255

These sections cover, in order above, the point that retired pay is not considered a pension, disability retirement, dual compensation, and disability compensation.

27C C.J.S. *Divorce* §557-559

General discussion on divorce and pensions. Military retirement pay, including disability, is covered.

American Jurisprudence, 2d

6 Am.Jur.2d *Attachment and Garnishment* §179.5

For those interested in reading the general law about garnishments, and how states have applied it.

24 Am. Jur. 2d *Divorce and Separation* §909 and §911 (1983 and Supp.)

These two sections discuss military retired pay and disability benefits, respectively. Only very general information is given on *McCarty*, with some of it somewhat incorrect. For example, the statement is made that "All valid court orders directing payment of a portion of retired pay to the nonmilitary spouse will be honored...if the divorcing couple was married for at least ten years during which the military spouse was in service." This statement fails to tell the reader that there are specific procedures that must be followed in order to receive payment, and other requirements must also be met.

American Law Reports

Annotation, *Pension or Retirement Benefits as Subject to Award or Division by Court in Settlement of Property Rights Between Spouses,* 94 A.L.R. 3d 176 (1979) & Supp.

Annotation, *Federal Pre-Emption of State Authority Over Domestic Relations—Federal Cases,* 70 L.Ed.2d 895 & Supp.

LEGAL PERIODICAL LITERATURE

Articles (in alphabetical order by author)

Cardos and Sinnott, *The Uniformed Services Former Spouses Protection Act.* 33 Fed. Bar. J. 33, January 1986.

Defense Department Would Not Oppose Divorce Bill If Changes made. 385 Pension Reporter 426 (March 22, 1982) (BNA). This article gives a good initial introduction to efforts to overturn *McCarty* and what led up to the USFSPA.

Guilford, *Uniformed Services Former Spouses' Protection Act Update,* Army Lawyer 43 (June 1989).

Henderson, *Dividing Military Retirement Pay and Disability Pay: A More Equitable Approach*, 134 Mil.L.Rev. 87 (Fall 1991).

Hochman, *The Supreme Court and the Constitutionality of Retroactive Legislation*, 73 Harv. L.R. 663 (1960). While not specifically addressing the issue as it relates to USFSPA, this article is, nonetheless, interesting in getting a perspective as to why retroactivity was not excluded in USFSPA initially.

MacIntyre, *A Legal Assistance Symposium—Division of U.S. Army Reserve and National Guard Pay Upon Divorce*, 102 Mil.L.Rev. 23 (Fall 1983). Despite the date of this article, the information is still current. The point that is raised is that the "hardships" and inequities that were originally cited as the main reason in changing the law do not exist when the military member is a reservist. The author examines in detail the "language" of the original statute to determine whether reservists were ever meant to fall under this law. Problems are created in calculating the eligibility for direct payment of retirement benefits.

Shiles, *The Second Legal Assistance Symposium—Part III: Legal Assistance Overseas: Rights of Family Members Who Separate While Residing in the Federal Republic of Germany*, 112 Mil. L. Rev. 131 (Spring 1986). This article discusses the basic rights of family members who separate from the military sponsor while residing in Germany.

Woldman, Elizabeth. *The Division of Military Pension Benefits in New Mexico in the Aftermath of Mansell.* Divorce Litigation, Vol. 1, No. 9, pp. S1 (3), November 1989.

WEST KEY-NUMBER DIGEST SYSTEM

Most of the cases in West digests can be found under the following Key Numbers, with the division of military retirement in a divorce appearing under "Divorce, 252.3."

Armed Services
 Key 13.5   Retirement pay and disability retirement
 Key 104   Compensation for disability

Divorce
 Key 248   Disposition of property
 Key 252   Division of property
 Key 252.3 Insurance, retirement, or pension rights

Husband and Wife
Key 240   Insurance & retirement benefits

11. *LEGISLATION — FEDERAL*

5 C.F.R. §581 — processing of garnishments for child support and/or alimony.

5 C.F.R. §831 — waiving military retirement in favor of a civil service pension based upon both periods of service combined.

32 C.F.R. §48 — sets forth procedures for administering the Retired Serviceman's Family Protection Plan (RSFPP), which was the forerunner of the Survivor Benefit Plan (SBP). (SBP replaced RSFPP in 1972.)

32 C.F.R. §63 — describes procedures for processing USFSPA direct payments. The address for each designated agent in each Uniformed Service is provided.

10 U.S.C. §1401 — states that military retirement pay is not a pension or annuity.

10 U.S.C. §1408 — Uniformed Services Former Spouses' Protection Act, Pub.L. 97-252, 96 Stat. 730 (1982). This is the initial Act, as part of the Department of Defense Authorization Act of 1983. It amends 10 U.S.C. §1002, Ch. 71.

10 U.S.C. §1448 (b)(2) and §1450(f) — sets forth eligibility requirements for members who may elect or are required to elect SBP for former spouses or to both a former spouse and child.

38 U.S.C. §3101 [amended by Pub.L. 99-576 §503 (October 28, 1986)] — permits the VA to deduct SBP costs from VA compensation when military retired pay is waived for such compensation.

42 U.S.C. §665 (1988) — involuntary allotments from pay for child and spousal support.

38 U.S.C. §1115, 1135 — additional VA compensation for dependents; if rated equal to or greater than 30 percent, the member gets additional money for dependents.

50 U.S.C. §501 et. seq. — Soldiers' and Sailors' Civil Relief Act of 1940. Whenever a servicemember is involved in a legal ac-

tion, certain rights must be complied with. (§513-Protection of persons secondarily liable; §520-Default Judgments; affidavits; bonds, attorneys for persons in service; §521-Stay of proceedings where military service affects conduct)

12. *LEGISLATIVE HISTORY*

Pre-1989 History:

S.2248 (H.R.6030):
House Reports: No. 97-482 accompanying H.R. 6030 (House Armed Services Committee) and No. 97-749 (Conference Committee).
Senate Report: No. 97-330 (Senate Armed Services Committee).
128 Cong.Rec. (1982): May 3-6, 11-13, considered and passed Senate. July 19-22, 27-29, H.R. 6030, considered and passed House; S.2248, amended, passed in lieu. Aug. 17, Senate agreed to conference report. Aug. 18, House agreed to conference report.

Hearings (information found in CIS)
H201-17 Benefits for Former Spouses of Military Members, 11/5/81. Committee Serial HASC No. 97-70 before Subcommittee on Military Personnel and Compensation to considered: H.R. 3039 (entitle spouses to pro rata share of military retirement), H.R. 1711 (require DoD compliance with state divorce court decisions), H.R. 1540 (authorize medical and dental care in DoD medical facilities for certain former spouses).

H.R. Rep. No. 749, 97th Cong, 2d Sess (reprinted in 1982 U.S. CODE CONG. & ADMIN NEWS, 1569-1573).

Other testimony:

Cong. Rec. 15721, (daily ed. July 14, 1981). H.R. 1711, H.R. 3039.

128 Cong.Rec. H4717 (daily ed. July 28, 1982) (reprinted in 1982 U.S. CODE CONG. & ADMIN NEWS, 1596). H.R. 6030 - the debate on FSPA.

S.Rep.No. 502, 1982 U.S. CODE CONG. & ADMIN NEWS, 1617.

Post-1989 Legislation:

H.R. 3525, introduced October 8, 1991, by Rep. Schroeder: a bill to apply the expanded definition of disposable retired pay to divorces retroactively. ARA believes that if the definition of disposable retired pay as defined in Public Law 101-510 were applied retroactively, military members (as well as their spouses) would have their divorce cases readjudicated where the parties had already agreed to the division in good faith.

H.R. 3915, introduced November 25, 1991, by Rep. Schroeder: a bill to amend 10 U.S.C. to provide commissary and exchange privileges to all former spouses who meet at least a 20/20/15 standard, regardless of the date of the divorce. If passed, former spouses would have more privileges than former military members who are now out of uniform and for whom such benefits were originally intended.

H.R. 4138, introduced January 29, 1992, by Rep. Schroeder: a bill to provide taxpayer-subsidized survivor benefits to certain former spouses of members who were eligible to participate but who did not or could not designate a former spouse as a beneficiary.

H.R. 2200, introduced May 2, 1991, by Rep. Dornan (see Chapter 12 and Appendix H).

[None of these 4 bills, introduced in the 102d Congress, was passed.]

Union List:

Other legislative history on USFSPA, Public Law 97-252, Department of Defense Authorization Act, 1983, 96 Sta. 730 can be obtained from the Union List of Legislative Histories, 5th ed., 47th Congress, 1881-98th Congress, 1984: Van Ness, Feldman, Sutcliffe, Curtis & Levenberg. (1050 Thomas Jefferson St. NW, Washington DC 20007; 202-331-9400.)

13. NATIONAL CENTER ON WOMEN & FAMILY LAW, INC.

799 Broadway, Room 402, New York, NY 10003 (212) 674-8200. This organization can provide information on women and pensions. It has a list of other organizations involved in pension issues, as well as a list of articles and pamphlets on the subject. They also have a fact sheet on federal laws with regard to spou-

sal interest in pensions (which includes military retirement pensions). They also publish the newsletter, *The Women's Advocate*. An article on USFSPA was written by Celentano and Avner, "Ex-Wives of Military Win as Congress Overturns McCarty v. McCarty," March 1983.

14. PERSONNEL OFFICES (AT MILITARY INSTALLATIONS)

The Military Personnel Office at the local military installation will usually have two offices that can assist with USFSPA information and SBP. Help is available either in the Retirement Section or the Personal Affairs Section.

Once retired, a military member will receive some newsletter from his service. For example, the Air Force publishes AFRP 30-16. "Afterburner—USAF News for Retired Personnel." The Army publishes "Army Echoes." Information on USFSPA and related matters is published in this recurring pamphlet, along with updates on legislation and telephone numbers for assistance with retiree matters.

15. SERVICE PROCEDURES & REGULATIONS

Each of the uniformed services has information or fact sheets at both USFSPA and SBP. In some cases, you may receive a copy of the procedures that you would have to follow when applying for benefits under either law. You can obtain information sheets from several sources—the active duty military personnel office, the base or post legal office, the retiree center (e.g., the Air Force's headquarters for retiree affairs is located at Randolph AFB in San Antonio, Texas), or the finance center. In 1992, the service finance centers were joined under one defense agency, the Defense Financing and Accounting Service.

The best aggregate source for information on the various finance centers is a book titled *Retired Military Almanac*. It is published annually by the Uniformed Services Almanac, Inc. Copies are usually sold in the military exchanges. They can also be ordered directly from the publisher [P.O. Box 4144, Falls Church, Virginia 22044. Telephone: (703) 532-1631].

If you want to call the finance center for information on either the USFSPA or SBP, you can usually do so via an 800 number. Each center has offices staffed with attorneys who specialize in either USFSPA or SBP. Be advised, however, that if you wish to speak directly with an attorney on a specific matter relating to either of these two topics, you will probably have to call them directly on a non toll-free line.

16. SPOUSES'S CLUBS

While not as closely knit as in the past, officer's and noncommissioned officer's civilian and military spouse clubs (formerly known as the Wives' Clubs) are available. At some locations, there may not be two separate clubs because there are not enough people or economics do not allow it. (In recent years, due to declining membership, many officer's clubs have now become "all ranks" clubs.) The mission is primarily social, but recently, due to the changing demographics of working spouses, membership activities are more oriented toward academic, charitable, and support issues.

Wives are learning more about the benefits available to them, and are less inclined to accept the status quo and be left "in the dark." A male military member who is going through a divorce should be aware that his spouse will probably know more about military retirement benefits to her in a divorce action than he will, precisely because of the educational programs that have sprung up in recent years.

17. SUPPORT GROUPS

More so today, there are many groups available to both the husband and wife when it comes to seeking help with domestic issues. Often, these groups, staffed primarily by volunteers, have a wealth of literature available, including statistical information. While women's groups are more prevalent, men's groups are starting to appear more and more.

Women usually have a wider choice from among numerous social, health, general support (e.g., battered wife, shelters), and associations. Men's choices have, until recently, been limited to the usual "single parent" organization and to divorce support groups. Within the last five years, however, men's awareness groups have begun to appear.

One very excellent source of support in coping with the trauma of divorce as well as the rebuilding process, are three programs sponsored by the Roman Catholic archdiocese called Coping, Rebuilding, and Beginning Experience. (You do not have to be Catholic to attend, and the programs are offered around the country.) Both men and women attend, and the support and learning that result can be worth savings of hundreds of dollars over one-on-one psychotherapy.

Many active duty military members are reluctant to go for professional help for fear of their security clearances or other reasons. Those who feel that way would be interested in programs such as these. The cost is either free (for Coping) or less than $50 for a 10-week seminar in Rebuilding. The text used in Rebuilding is one of the most comprehensive books one will ever come across in explaining the entire emotional process of divorce.

The local community may sponsor a number of workshops or information sessions or publish information related to divorce and divorce issues.

The following is a sampling in the Washington DC metropolitan area: (1) Fairfax County Commission on Women (Virginia); (2) The Women's Center, Vienna, Virginia. Tel: (703) 281-2657; (3) The Divorce and Counseling Center of Montgomery County (MD).

The following groups are in the Albuquerque NM area (the area code is the same for all numbers—505): (1) Divorce/Separation Group. Call Beth, 884-9411. (2) Affairs—Understand Their Meaning, for those whose relationships were disrupted by an affair. 822-8210. (3) Dads Against Discrimination, Inc., 299-COPE. (4) Divorce and Separation Group. Call Michelle, 247-9521. (5) Domestic Violence (Victims and Victim Survivors). 839-0520, 292-8290. (6) Domestic Violence Legal Hotline. 843-8800. Outside Albuquerque (but in NM), 1-800-288-3854. (7) F.A.T.H.E.R.S. (Fathers Attempting To Have Equal Rights). 857-1522. (8) Manline (hotline for family crisis referrals, emphasis on assisting men). 892-5489. (9) Divorce support, Monday evenings at 5 p.m., First United Methodist Church, 4th and Lead SW; non-denominational discussion groups. No charge; nursery.

18. SURVIVOR BENEFIT PLAN (SBP)

The Retired Officers Association publishes an excellent booklet entitled "SBP Made Easy." It costs less than $5 and is available from TROA, 201 N. Washington St. Alexandria VA 22314-2539. Tel: 1-800-245-TROA, (703) 549-2311. The publication has an extensive section on the Social Security Offset issue. It can serve as a basic guide for retirement planning, particularly in estimating financial interests. (However, the reader should be aware that changes to SBP are frequent, and they often involve the offset issue, making long-term financial planning less sure, if one is seeking a bottom-line dollar amount.) The guide is also helpful in presenting the facts regarding SBP coverage when you waive military retired pay in favor of a combined military/civil service retirement.

The Army Air Force Mutual Aid Association (AAFMA), located on Ft. Myer in Arlington, Virginia (Tel: 1-800-336-4538), was founded 114 years ago to ensure that all active, reserve, and retired officers receive the benefits to which they are entitled. AAFMA works with each member who is reviewing various financial or separation (from service) options to provide free unbiased life insurance counseling (as well as other pre-retirement/separation-from-service counseling), and detailed forecasts of the effect on your benefits, including options relative to SBP. You can receive information on what your projected costs will be, and what the value of the SBP is to the spouse. They also provide a number of other estate planning services, and are well worth the fee to join. If you are an active reservist (in a billet), the services AAFMA provides can be invaluable, including keeping track of your accumulated retirement points. (Unfortunately, if you are an active reservist in a non-pay category, you are not eligible to join AAFMA. We would like to see AAFMA revise its membership policy to include all reservists, whether in a pay billet or non-pay status.)

This resource listing is but a small compilation of reference materials. If you know of other sources that should be included, please let the authors know.

ORDER FORM

QUANTITY	PRODUCT	PRICE	COST
	Book: DIVORCE AND THE MILITARY	14.95 each	(1)
	ARA Member Discount (on books only): 10% for 1-9 books; 20% for 10+:		(2)
	Computation Chart for Net Disposable Retirement Shares: ___ pre-1991 divorce ($1.50) ___ post-1990 divorce ($1.50) ___ both ($2)		(3)
	Full Text of USFSPA law: ___ 1-2 copies ($2.50 each) ___ 3-5 copies ($2.00 each) ___ 6+ ($1.75 each)		(4)
	Shipping & Handling---books (check one): ___ Surface Rate (2-4 wks): $2.50 for first book; $1.75 for each additional book. ___ First Class (2-5 days): $3.75 for first book; $2.25 for each additional book.		(5)
	Shipping & Handling---charts & text: ___ First Class: 1-2 cy charts, $.50; $.35 each additional copy ___ First Class: 1 cy USFSPA law, $.75; $.45 each additional copy		(6)
	15% additional postage (on lines 5 + 6) for foreign addresses (excluding APOs):		(7)
	Subtotal (lines 1 - 2 + 3 + 4 + 5 + 6 + 7):		(8)
	California & New Mexico residents add applicable sales tax for amount on line (8):		(9)
	TOTAL ENCLOSED check or money order for total (lines 8 + 9):		$

— OVER —

207

MAIL FORM TO: ARA, P.O. Box 1424, Bonsall, CA 92003-1424. *Sorry—no cash, telephone, fax, or credit card orders.*

Name(print) _____ Rank/Rate _____

Company/Organization _____ Telephone (___) _____

Address _____ City/State _____

ZIP+4 _____

Please take a moment to check your status in each column, as applicable:

___ USAF	___ Active Duty	___ Officer
___ USA	___ Retired	___ Enlisted
___ USMC	___ Reserve/Guard	___ Warrant Officer
___ USN	___ Retired Reserve/Guard	___ Officer (prior enlisted)
___ USCG	___ Spouse of Active Duty	___ Other Dependent
___ PHS	___ Spouse of Retiree	___ Lawyer (___ Former JAG)
___ NOAA	___ Spouse of Reserve/Guard	___ Other _____

ARA Membership Application

Dues $25/year (includes bi-monthly newsletter)	$
Contribution	
Pledge Monthly _____	
Canada/Foreign addresses add $10/year (for postage)	
TOTAL AMOUNT ENCLOSED (check or money order)	$

Dues and contributions are tax deductible.
Send check or money order and form to ARA corporate headquarters:

ARA
P.O. Box 1424
Bonsall, CA 92003-1424

Name (please print)_____
Rank/Rate _____Male_____Female_____
Company/Organization_____
Address_____
City/State_____
ZIP+4_____
Telephone (____)_____(Day___Evening___)

Please check your status in each column, as applicable:

____USAF	____Active Duty	____Officer
____USA	____Retired	____Enlisted
____USMC	____Reserve/Guard	____Warrant Officer
____USN	____Retired Reserve/Guard	____Officer (prior enlisted)
____USCG	____Spouse of Active Duty	____Other Dependent
____PHS	____Spouse of Retiree	____Lawyer(___former JAG)
____NOAA	____Spouse of Reserve/Guard	____Other_____

Mail inquiries relating to dues, membership, and publications to the California office. Direct all other matters to:

ARA Washington Operations Office
2009 N. 14th St., Ste. 300
Arlington, VA 22201-2514
Telephone (703) 527-3065   Fax (703) 528-4229

OFFICE USE:

RCA_____

CMO_____